Cookies BEST BBQ RECIPES

Meredith® Books
Des Moines, Iowa

Cookies Best BBQ Recipes
by Speed Herrig

Editor: Stephanie Karpinske
Contributing Editor: Janet Figg
Designer: Erin Burns
Contributing Designer: Joyce DeWitt
Copy Chief: Terri Fredrickson
Publishing Operations Manager: Karen Schirm
Edit and Design Production Coordinator: Mary Lee Gavin
Editorial Assistants: Cheryl Eckert, Kairee Windsor
Marketing Product Managers: Aparna Pande, Isaac Petersen,
    Gina Rickert, Stephen Rogers, Brent Wiersma, Tyler Woods
Book Production Managers: Pam Kvitne, Marjorie J.
    Schenkelberg, Rick von Holdt, Mark Weaver
Contributing Copy Editor: Sarah Oliver Watson
Contributing Proofreaders: Callie Dunbar, Susan J. Kling,
    Stacie McKee
Cover Photographer: Andy Lyons
Cover Food Stylist: Paige Boyle
Indexer: Spectrum Communication Services, Inc.

Meredith® Books
Executive Director, Editorial: Gregory H. Kayko
Executive Director, Design: Matt Strelecki
Senior Editor/Group Manager: Jan Miller
Senior Associate Design Director: Mick Schnepf

Publisher and Editor in Chief: James D. Blume
Editorial Director: Linda Raglan Cunningham
Executive Director, Marketing: Jeffrey B. Myers
Executive Director, New Business Development:
    Todd M. Davis
Executive Director, Sales: Ken Zagor
Director, Operations: George A. Susral
Director, Production: Douglas M. Johnston
Business Director: Jim Leonard

Vice President and General Manager: Douglas J. Guendel

Meredith Publishing Group
President: Jack Griffin
Senior Vice President: Bob Mate

Meredith Corporation
Chairman and Chief Executive Officer: William T. Kerr
President and Chief Operating Officer: Stephen M. Lacy

In Memoriam: E.T. Meredith III (1933-2003)

Copyright © 2005 by Meredith Corporation, Des Moines, Iowa. First Edition.
All rights reserved. Printed in China.
Library of Congress Control Number: 2004112903
ISBN: 0-696-22320-1

All of us at Meredith® Books are dedicated to providing you with the information and ideas you need to create delicious foods. We welcome your comments and suggestions. Write to us at: Meredith Books, Cookbook Editorial Department, 1716 Locust St., Des Moines, IA 50309-3023.

If you would like to purchase any of our cooking, crafts, gardening, home improvement, or home decorating and design books, check wherever quality books are sold. Or visit us at: meredithbooks.com

TABLE OF CONTENTS

The Story of COOKIES

L.D. Cook (nicknamed Cookie) made the first batch of **COOKIES Bar-B-Q Sauce** in his kitchen in 1975 in the small town of Wall Lake, Iowa. The sauce was so popular with local residents that Cook formed **COOKIES Food Products, Inc**. A year later, Speed Herrig, another local Wall Lake resident, met up with Cook and hit the road selling Cookies sauce out of the back of his pickup. His hard work and persistence paid off. In 1984 Herrig bought the company from Cook. At that time the sauce was being bottled in a small building on the edge of town.

Today Cookies products are still produced in Wall Lake, but Herrig and the Cookies crew are housed in an ultramodern 105,000 square foot manufacturing facility. It even has a test kitchen to try out new items and create recipes using Cookies products. This kitchen is also used to test recipes received from customers.

From its humble beginnings, the COOKIES product line, now available in 32 states, has grown to include three flavors of Bar-B-Q Sauce:

COOKIES Original—a sweet, smoky sauce

COOKIES Western Style—a zesty mix with onion and cayenne pepper

COOKIES Country Blend—a tangy blend with mustard paste and extra vinegar

Other COOKIES products include:

COOKIES Wings-N-Things Hot Sauce—excellent for buffalo-style chicken wings

COOKIES Taco Sauce & Dip—for tacos, chips, and more

COOKIES Mild and Medium Premium Salsas —to spice up all your favorite dishes

COOKIES Flavor Enhancer All-Purpose Seasoning—a dry mixture of secret ingredients that can be sprinkled on everything from meat to vegetables to popcorn.

This cookbook includes great recipes that feature all of the COOKIES products. From tasty appetizers to hearty main dishes, there's something for everyone. You'll also find helpful cooking tips to make each meal a success. And if you have a favorite recipe to share using one of our products, send it our way, addressed to:

COOKIES Food Products

P.O. Box 458

Wall Lake, Iowa 51466

Or e-mail Speed at:

speed@cookiesbbq.com

Can't find Cookies products at your favorite store? Then buy them online at ***www.cookiesbbq.com***.

the "SAUCEMAN" says Grilling Tips

COOKIES Bar-B-Q Sauces make food taste terrific no matter how you cook it, as you'll see when you sample the recipes in this book. Of all the ways to cook for family and friends, grilling is America's favorite. We love the ease of grilling and the tender, juicy foods it produces. When you fire up your grill, it's easy to get delicious results simply by brushing meat or chicken with one of the COOKIES Bar-B-Q Sauces. Here are some sure-fire tips to help you be a grillmaster.

Direct or indirect cooking?

With direct grilling, the food goes on the grill rack directly over the heat. Choose this method for foods that are tender, small or thin, and cook in less than 20 minutes—steaks, burgers, kabobs, hot dogs, boneless poultry, fish, and most vegetables. Indirect grilling—done with the grill cover down—is best for cooking whole chickens or turkeys, ribs, roasts, whole fish, and vegetables such as potatoes and corn on the cob.

When grilling indirect, resist the urge to peek. Every time you lift the lid, heat escapes and you add as much as 15 minutes to the cooking time. Let the foods cook the minimum time given in the recipe or chart before checking for doneness.

Be safe

Never use gasoline or kerosene to start charcoal. Use fire-starter gels as directed and never apply starters to an existing fire or even warm coals.

Take raw burgers and chicken to the grill on a clean plate. After cooking, place them on another clean plate to serve.

Don't guess about doneness. Use a meat thermometer or instant-read thermometer to be sure.

Steaks & chops

Turning meat too often is a waste of time. For direct grilling, turning once halfway through cooking is enough. When cooking indirect, you usually don't need to turn the meat at all.

Use tongs, not a fork, for turning so juices aren't lost through holes poked in the meat.

Burgers

Use good quality ground meat but not the leanest available. A little fat makes burgers moist and juicy.

For uniform patties, use a measuring cup or ice cream scoop to scoop up the meat mixture.

Shape the patties gently; don't squeeze or pack the meat.

Never press down on burgers with a spatula while they grill. This squeezes out the juices, making them tough and dry.

To ensure food safety, burgers should be cooked until well done.

Chicken & turkey

If you don't care for poultry skin, remove it before cooking or buy skinless pieces. However, the skin adds flavor and keeps the surface of the chicken from drying out during cooking. You can remove the skin after cooking if you're concerned about the fat it contains.

When grilling skinless chicken pieces, prevent sticking by spraying the cold rack with nonstick cooking spray or brushing lightly with cooking oil. Do this before grilling fish steaks and fillets, too.

Cook a turkey on the grill once and you'll never do it any other way, fans say. For best results, choose a turkey that weighs less than 16 pounds; larger birds are too big for some grills and may be difficult to remove from the grill. Only grill unstuffed turkeys because they cook more evenly than stuffed birds.

When grilling a whole chicken or turkey, you can place it on a rack in a roasting pan and omit the drip pan.

Fish

Fish is more fragile than meat or poultry so use a grill basket or place the fish on the grill on a double layer of heavy foil with slits cut in the foil.

Pieces of fish that are less than 1 inch thick don't need to be turned during grilling. Pieces that are 1 inch or thicker should be turned once about halfway through grilling, using a wide spatula.

Kabobs

Metal skewers are easier to use than wooden skewers, which will burn if not soaked in water for 30 minutes before using.

For even cooking, allow a $1/4$-inch space between food pieces on skewers.

Precook vegetables such as tiny whole potatoes and carrots before placing on skewers. Sweet pepper pieces, onion wedges, zucchini pieces, and mushrooms do not need to be precooked. Tomatoes cook quickly so add them only for the last few minutes of grilling time.

Vegetables

Grilling vegetables in packets made from folded heavy foil is a trade off. Packets are convenient

and cleanup is easy, but you sacrifice that delicious fresh-from-the-grill flavor.

A grilling basket, tray, or wok will give you that grilled flavor works well for small or cut-up vegetables, with no worry about food falling into the fire. Or if you don't have one of those, use a foil pan.

Using wood chips

Wood chips give foods an appetizing wood-smoked aroma and flavor. Good chip choices include mesquite, hickory, oak, and sweet fruitwoods, such as apple, cherry, and peach. Supermarkets that stock charcoal usually carry wood chips as well, or order from websites.

For large meat cuts and whole birds that take longer to cook, use wood chunks, which last longer than chips.

Soak chips or chunks in enough water to cover for at least 1 hour before using. For long cooking times, soak enough wood to add more to the grill as necessary.

When using a charcoal grill, sprinkle drained chips on the coals. For a gas grill, place chips in a metal box, disposable foil pan, or wrap in heavy foil with holes poked in the top for steam to escape.

If you have fresh herbs in your garden, use them to flavor the smoke. Add a generous handful to the coals when you put the food on the rack.

Cleaning up

Cleaning the grill after each use helps prevent flare-ups next time.

After each use of your gas grill, turn the grill settings to high for 10 to 15 minutes with the lid closed. Then simply brush off the grill rack using a brass bristle brush.

For a charcoal grill, remove the grill rack and wrap it in wet newspaper. Let it stand about 1 hour, then wipe it clean. If necessary, use a stiff brush to remove stubborn burned-on food.

APPETIZERS SAUCES & MARINADES

Chapter 1

BBQ Brats & Kraut

2   cups brats that have been grilled,
      skinned, and chopped
¾   cup COOKIES Original Bar-B-Q Sauce
1   8-oz. can sauerkraut, drained
1   tbsp. Worcestershire sauce
1   tbsp. garlic powder
1   tbsp. ground cumin
1   tsp. yellow mustard
    Shredded mozzarella cheese
    Crackers
    Snipped fresh parsley
    Cherry tomatoes

1. In a medium bowl, mix chopped brats, Bar-B-Q Sauce, sauerkraut, Worcestershire sauce, garlic powder, cumin, and mustard and let marinate in refrigerator for 2 to 3 hours. Place in a 2-quart rectangular dish and microwave, covered, on 100% power (high) for 2 minutes. Stir and cook 2 minutes more. Top with mozzarella cheese and serve on crackers. Garnish platter with parsley and cherry tomatoes.
Makes: 10 to 12 servings

Bite-Size Meat Snacks

2   5- to 6-oz. boneless pork chops,
      ¾ to 1 inch thick
2   skinless, boneless chicken breast halves
1   8-oz. boneless beef sirloin steak,
      1 inch thick
    COOKIES Flavor Enhancer
    COOKIES Original Bar-B-Q Sauce

1. Season pork, chicken, and beef with Flavor Enhancer. Grill directly over medium coals, turning once. Allow 12 to 15 minutes for pork (160°); 12 to 15 minutes for chicken (170°); and for beef allow 14 to 18 minutes for medium rare (145°) or 18 to 20 minutes for medium (160°). Cut into bite-size pieces.

2. Have 2 or 3 flavors of COOKIES Bar-B-Q Sauces in small bowls. Serve with toothpicks.
Makes: 16 servings

Easy Meatballs

2	lbs. ground beef
1¼	cups soft bread crumbs
¾	cup milk
2	eggs
1	pkg. onion soup mix
¼	tsp. COOKIES Flavor Enhancer
2	tbsp. cooking oil
2	cups COOKIES Original Bar-B-Q Sauce
½	cup shredded cheddar cheese

1. Combine beef, bread crumbs, milk, eggs, onion soup mix, and Flavor Enhancer in a large bowl. Shape into 1½-inch meatballs. Heat oil in a 12-inch skillet and brown meatballs on all sides over medium heat. Drain and place in a 2-quart baking dish. Cover with Bar-B-Q Sauce. Bake, uncovered, in a 350° oven for 45 minutes. Top with cheese. Return to oven for 5 minutes to melt cheese.
Makes: 16 to 20 servings

Manhattan Meatballs

1½	lbs. ground beef
½	lb. ground pork
2	cups soft bread crumbs
2	eggs, lightly beaten
½	cup chopped onion
2	tbsp. dried parsley flakes
1	tsp. COOKIES Flavor Enhancer
2	tbsp. cooking oil
1	small jar apricot preserves
1	cup COOKIES Original Bar-B-Q Sauce

1. Combine beef, pork, bread crumbs, eggs, onion, parsley, and Flavor Enhancer. Shape into 1½-inch meatballs. Heat oil in a 12-inch skillet and brown meatballs on all sides over medium heat. Drain and place in 2-quart baking dish. Combine preserves and Bar-B-Q Sauce. Cover meatballs with sauce mixture and bake, uncovered, in a 350° oven for 45 minutes.
Makes: 16 to 20 servings

Note: If desired, use a small jar of grape jelly in place of apricot preserves.

the "SAUCEMAN" says

Try using crushed soda crackers in place of bread crumbs for meatballs. Or use graham crackers for a sweeter taste.

Porcupine Meatballs

1½   lbs. ground beef
½   lb. ground pork
1½   cups cooked rice
1   small onion, diced
½   cup milk
2   tbsp. diced green sweet pepper
1   tsp. dried parsley flakes
½   tsp. COOKIES Flavor Enhancer
2   tbsp. cooking oil
1½   cups COOKIES Original Bar-B-Q Sauce

1. Combine beef, pork, rice, onion, milk, green pepper, parsley, and Flavor Enhancer in a large bowl. Shape into 1½-inch balls. Heat oil in a 12-inch skillet and brown meatballs on all sides over medium heat. Drain fat. Place in baking dish and cover with Bar-B-Q Sauce. Bake, covered, in a 350° oven for 1 hour.

Makes: 16 to 20 servings

the "SAUCEMAN" says

For meatballs with a twist, use crushed cornflakes or corn bread instead of bread crumbs. Or use onion-flavored potato chips.

Vegetable Meatballs

1   lb. ground beef
1   egg
¾   cup grated raw potato
¾   cup grated raw carrots
½   cup chopped celery
1   onion, chopped
1   cup uncooked Minute Rice
¼   tsp. COOKIES Flavor Enhancer
2   tbsp. cooking oil
     COOKIES Original Bar-B-Q Sauce

1. Combine ground beef, egg, potato, carrots, celery, onion, rice, and Flavor Enhancer. Shape into 1-inch meatballs. Heat oil in a 12-inch skillet and brown meatballs on all sides over medium heat. Drain fat. Drizzle Bar-B-Q Sauce over the meatballs. Bring to boiling; reduce heat. Simmer, covered, for 45 minutes.

Makes: 12 to 16 servings

Cocktail Meatballs

1   lb. ground beef

1   lb. ground smoked ham

½   lb. ground pork

2   eggs

2   cups wheat cereal flakes, crushed

1   cup milk or half-and-half

1   tsp. COOKIES Flavor Enhancer

2   cups COOKIES Original Bar-B-Q Sauce

½   cup water

¼   cup raspberry jam

1. Combine beef, ham, pork, eggs, crushed cereal, milk, and Flavor Enhancer. Shape into 1-inch meatballs. Place in a single layer in a 3-quart rectangular baking dish. Combine Bar-B-Q Sauce, water, and jam. Bring to a boil. Pour the sauce mixture over the meatballs. Bake, uncovered, in a 350° oven for 1 hour.

Makes: 20 to 24 servings

COOKIES Bar-B-Q Cups

1   lb. ground beef

½   cup COOKIES Original Bar-B-Q Sauce

2   tbsp. packed brown sugar

1   tsp. minced onion

½   tsp. COOKIES Flavor Enhancer

1   10-count pkg. refrigerated biscuits

¼   cup shredded cheddar cheese

¼   cup shredded mozzarella cheese

1. Brown ground beef and drain. Add Bar-B-Q Sauce, brown sugar, onion, and Flavor Enhancer. Press biscuits into muffin cups and spoon in Bar-B-Q Sauce mixture. Top with cheeses. Bake in a 350° oven for 20 minutes.

Makes: 10 servings

Beef Jerky

2   lbs. beef, cut into thin strips
½   cup Worcestershire sauce
½   cup soy sauce
3   tbsp. coarse black pepper
2   tbsp. liquid smoke
2   tbsp. garlic powder

1. Combine all ingredients in a shallow baking dish. Cover and marinate in refrigerator for 3 to 4 days. Drain beef well and pat dry with paper towels. Spread in a single layer on baking sheets. Bake in a 150° oven for 5 to 8 hours or until dry.
Makes: 12 servings

COOKIES Southwestern Nacho Round

1   16-oz. pkg. hot roll mix
1   lb. lean ground beef, crumbled
1   pkg. onion soup mix
½   cup water
1½   cups COOKIES Premium Salsa
1   tsp. fajita seasoning
½   tsp. ground cumin
1   16-oz. can refried beans
1   cup Cheese 'N Salsa
2   oz. Colby cheese, shredded (½ cup)
½   cup green chiles, chopped and drained
½   cup pitted ripe olives, chopped and drained
     Dairy sour cream
     COOKIES Premium Salsa

1. Prepare hot roll mix according to package directions. While dough rests, in a large skillet combine beef, soup mix, and water; cook until meat is browned. Drain. Add Premium Salsa, fajita seasoning, and cumin. Heat until bubbly. Remove from heat.

2. Roll dough on a lightly floured surface to an 18-inch circle; place on a greased large pizza pan. Spread refried beans in a 10-inch circle in center of dough. Top with ground beef mixture, Cheese 'N Salsa, Colby cheese, green chiles, and olives. With pastry scissors or a sharp knife, cut into dough forming 2-inch-wide strips about 1 inch from filling. Lap the strips over each other.

3. Bake in a 375° oven for 20 to 25 minutes or until crust is done (bottom is golden). Cool for 10 minutes. Place on a large serving platter. Garnish with sour cream and more Premium Salsa. Cut into wedges and serve.
Makes: 8 servings

COOKIES Nacho Supreme

1½ lbs. ground beef
1 large onion, chopped
½ cup COOKIES Taco Sauce & Dip
    Dash COOKIES Wings-N-Things Hot Sauce
1 16-oz. can refried beans
½ cup sliced pitted ripe olives
2 cups shredded cheddar cheese
1 cup shredded lettuce
2 tomatoes, chopped
½ cup dairy sour cream
½ cup guacamole
1 pkg. nacho cheese chips

1. Brown ground beef and onion in a large skillet; drain fat. Stir in Taco Sauce and Wings-N-Things. Spoon refried beans in the bottom of a 2-quart baking dish. Top with the ground beef mixture. Sprinkle with olives and cheese and bake, uncovered, in a 350° oven for 20 minutes.

2. Top with lettuce, tomatoes, sour cream, and guacamole. Place chips around edge of baking dish and serve hot.
Makes: 12 to 16 servings

"SAUCEMAN" says

Run cottage cheese through a blender for a healthier sour cream substitute. Flavor it with chives, relishes, and extracts, and use it in place of mayonnaise as well.

Party Pizzas

¾ lb. ground beef
1 small onion, chopped
1 7½-oz. tube (10) refrigerated biscuits
1 cup COOKIES Original Bar-B-Q Sauce
½ cup shredded cheddar cheese
½ cup shredded mozzarella cheese

1. Brown ground beef and onion in a medium skillet. Drain and set aside to cool slightly. Remove biscuits from tube and flatten slightly with hands. Place on a lightly greased cookie sheet. Cover biscuits with Bar-B-Q Sauce. Top Bar-B-Q Sauce with ground beef and shredded cheeses. Bake in a 350° oven for 8 to 10 minutes.
Makes: 10 servings

Buffalo Wings

12   chicken wings

3   tbsp. butter or margarine

¼   cup all-purpose flour

1   tbsp. white vinegar

2   to 3 tsp. COOKIES Wings-N-Things Hot Sauce

¼   tsp. COOKIES Flavor Enhancer

1. Cut off and discard tips of chicken wings. Cut wings at joints to form 24 pieces.

2. Melt 2 tablespoons of the butter or margarine in a 13×9×2-inch baking pan in a 425° oven. Coat wings with flour and place in pan. Bake, uncovered, for 20 minutes. Turn and bake for 20 to 25 minutes more. Remove from oven and drain on paper towels. Melt remaining 1 tablespoon butter and combine in a large bowl with vinegar, Wings-N-Things, and Flavor Enhancer. Add baked wings. Toss until evenly coated.
Makes: 12 servings

Caliente Chicken Wings

8   chicken wings

1   cup milk

1   egg

1   cup flour

2   tsp. ground cumin

½   tsp. cayenne pepper

2   cups cooking oil

½   cup COOKIES Taco Sauce & Dip, warmed

1. Cut off and discard tips of chicken wings. Cut wings at joints.

2. Beat milk and egg thoroughly in a small bowl. Dip wings into milk mixture to coat lightly. Mix flour, cumin, and cayenne in a plastic bag. Place wings in bag and shake. Refrigerate for 30 minutes. Heat oil in an electric fry pan (or a large skillet with sides at least 2 inches deep) to 400°. Fry chicken wings for 7 minutes or until golden brown. Drain on paper towels. Arrange on a plate and cover with warmed Taco Sauce. Serve immediately.
Makes: 8 servings

Honey-Glazed Drumsticks or Wings

½   cup butter (1 stick)

6   chicken drumsticks or 12 chicken wings

¼   to ⅓ cup honey
    COOKIES Flavor Enhancer

1. Melt butter in a 13×9×2-inch baking pan. Add drumsticks or wings; turn to coat. Pour enough honey over chicken to lightly coat. Season with Flavor Enhancer. Bake, uncovered, in a 350° oven for 20 minutes. Turn chicken over and coat with remaining honey and additional Flavor Enhancer. Bake for 20 minutes more or until chicken is done.

Makes: 6 servings

Mexican Cluckers

18   chicken wings (about 3 lbs.)

1   18-oz. bottle COOKIES Original Bar-B-Q Sauce

1   small onion, chopped

2   cloves garlic, minced

½   cup raisins

½   tsp. COOKIES Flavor Enhancer

1   tbsp. chili powder

½   tsp. ground cinnamon

¼   tsp. ground cloves

1. Cut off and discard tips of chicken wings. Cut wings at joints to form 36 pieces. Place wings in a large plastic bag set in a large bowl.

2. In a blender combine Bar-B-Q Sauce, onion, garlic, raisins, Flavor Enhancer, chili powder, cinnamon, and cloves; blend until almost smooth. Pour over the chicken in bag. Seal bag and refrigerate overnight.

3. Place chicken and sauce in a shallow roasting pan. Bake, uncovered, in a 300° oven for 1 hour.

Makes: 18 servings

Goober Balls

1   lb. uncooked ground turkey

1   lb. uncooked ground chicken

1   cup finely chopped onion

1   cup crushed crackers

½   tsp. COOKIES Flavor Enhancer

1   egg, beaten

1   18-oz. bottle COOKIES Original
    Bar-B-Q Sauce

1. Combine turkey, chicken, onion, crackers, Flavor Enhancer, and egg in a large bowl. Shape into 16 balls. Place in a 3½- to 4-quart slow cooker. Cover and cook on high-heat setting for 2 hours. Carefully drain any excess fat. Pour on Bar-B-Q Sauce. Cover and cook for 1 to 2 hours or until an instant-read thermometer inserted into a meatball reads 165°.
Makes: 16 servings

Pollosticks

1   8-oz. carton dairy sour cream
    chive-flavored dip

¼   cup COOKIES Taco Sauce & Dip

1   tbsp. finely chopped onion

½   tsp. garlic salt

10 chicken wings

½   cup COOKIES Taco Sauce & Dip

¼   cup butter, melted

½   cup all-purpose flour

½   tsp. paprika

½   tsp. COOKIES Flavor Enhancer

¼   tsp. Italian seasoning, crushed

2   cups cooking oil

1. Combine sour cream, ¼ cup Taco Sauce, onion, and garlic salt in a small bowl. Cover and chill.

2. Cut off and discard tips of chicken wings. Cut wings at joints to form 20 pieces. In bowl, combine ½ cup Taco Sauce and melted butter. In a plastic bag, combine flour, paprika, Flavor Enhancer, and Italian seasoning. Dip wings in butter mixture, then dredge in the flour mixture. Place oil in an electric skillet or large skillet with sides at least 2 inches deep. Heat oil to 375°. Fry wings in hot oil about 7 minutes or until golden brown. Remove and drain on paper towels. Serve with chilled sour cream mixture.
Makes: 10 servings

Deluxe Cocktail Smokies

2 lbs. cocktail smokies
1 12-oz. can beer
1 26-oz. bottle COOKIES Bar-B-Q Sauce
   (your favorite flavor)

1. Simmer cocktail smokies in beer in a large saucepan about 20 minutes; drain. Add Bar-B-Q Sauce. Reheat in pan or slow cooker.
Makes: 12 servings

Drunken Dogs

1 cup packed brown sugar
1 cup bourbon
1 cup COOKIES Taco Sauce & Dip
2 lbs. hot dogs, cut in ½-inch pieces

1. In a 3½ - to 4-quart slow cooker, combine brown sugar, bourbon, and Taco Sauce. Add hot dogs; cover and cook on low-heat setting for 4 to 6 hours.
Makes: 16 servings

Note: May use whiskey in place of the bourbon. May use COOKIES Original Bar-B-Q Sauce in place of the Taco Sauce. Goes great with corn chips.

the "SAUCEMAN" says

To remedy rock-hard brown sugar, add a slice of bread to the package and close the bag tightly. The sugar will be soft again in a few hours.

Oriental Ribs

2 lbs. pork back ribs, sawed in half crosswise

¼ cup soy sauce

¼ cup Wings-N-Things Hot Sauce

2 tbsp. honey

2 tbsp. sake, dry wine, or apple juice

2 cloves garlic, crushed

1. Cut pork between ribs into 1½-inch pieces. Place pork in a shallow baking dish. Mix rest of ingredients and spoon over pork. Cover and refrigerate for 2 to 24 hours. Heat oven to 325°. Line baking dish with foil. Lay pork ribs, meaty side up, in lined baking dish. Brush with marinade. Bake, covered, for 1 hour. Remove and brush with marinade. Return to oven and bake, uncovered, for 45 minutes.

Makes: 12 servings

Taco Biscuits

1 lb. ground pork

3 cups shredded cheddar cheese

¾ cup COOKIES Taco Sauce & Dip

3 cups packaged biscuit mix

1 cup crushed corn chips

1. Brown ground pork in a large skillet; drain fat. Stir in cheese and Taco Sauce. Mix well. Add biscuit mix and blend well. Form into 1-inch balls. Roll in crushed corn chips. Place on a cookie sheet. Bake in a 450° oven for 15 minutes.

Makes: 12 servings

Shrimp Appetizer

36	large cooked shrimp
1	tbsp. lemon juice
1	tbsp. Worcestershire sauce
1½	cups COOKIES Original Bar-B-Q Sauce
18	slices turkey bacon
⅓	cup shredded Monterey Jack cheese

1. Peel and devein shrimp. Mix lemon juice, Worcestershire sauce, and ½ cup of the Bar-B-Q Sauce. Place shrimp in mixture and marinate in refrigerator for 4 hours. Cut bacon strips in halves. Partially fry bacon. Do not overcook. Drain on paper towels. Wrap each piece of shrimp with a halved bacon strip. Broil wrapped shrimp 3 to 4 inches from heat for 5 minutes or until bacon is done, turning as needed. Secure shrimp with toothpicks. Dip each shrimp in remaining 1 cup Bar-B-Q Sauce. Place shrimp on a microwavable serving tray. Sprinkle shrimp with cheese. Cover and refrigerate. Heat shrimp in microwave prior to serving. Serve hot.

Makes: 36 servings

Shrimp Canapes

1	4-oz. can shrimp
¼	cup butter, softened
¼	cup diced onion
¼	cup COOKIES Taco Sauce & Dip
2	tbsp. diced green chile peppers
1	tbsp. lemon juice
½	tsp. yellow mustard
½	tsp. Worcestershire sauce
	Dash COOKIES Flavor Enhancer
	Crackers or small party breads

1. Drain shrimp and chop finely. Stir together butter, onion, Taco Sauce, chile peppers, lemon juice, mustard, Worcestershire sauce, and Flavor Enhancer. Gently stir in shrimp. Spread on crackers or bread.

Makes: 16 servings

Beef Dip

2   lbs. ground beef or ground pork
1   onion, chopped
1½ cups COOKIES Taco Sauce & Dip
1   11-oz. can condensed fiesta nacho
        cheese soup
1   lb. Velveeta cheese, cubed
    Tortilla chips

1. Brown beef with onion in a 12-inch skillet. Drain fat. Add Taco Sauce, soup, and cheese. Heat until cheese melts. Transfer to a serving bowl. Serve with tortilla chips.
Makes: 24 servings

Black Bean Dip

1   10½-oz. can black bean soup
1   cup COOKIES Taco Sauce & Dip
½   cup shredded cheddar cheese
¼   tsp. chili powder
    Corn chips

1. Combine soup, Taco Sauce, cheese, and chili powder in a saucepan and heat on low, stirring constantly. Serve hot with corn chips.
Makes: 12 servings

COOKIES Taco Dip

1   18-oz. bottle COOKIES Taco Sauce & Dip
1   8-oz. pkg. cream cheese, softened
1   16-oz. can refried beans
1   10-oz. pkg. shredded Colby cheese
3   large tomatoes, chopped
2   bunches green onions, chopped
1   2¼-oz. can sliced pitted ripe olives
    Corn chips

1. Stir together Taco Sauce and cream cheese until mixture is smooth. Evenly spread the refried beans on a 12-inch platter, then spread cream cheese and Taco Sauce mixture over beans. Layer with Colby cheese, tomatoes, green onions, and olives. Refrigerate until chilled. Serve with corn chips.
Makes: 12 servings

Avocado Dip

4   avocados

½   cup COOKIES Premium Salsa

½   cup COOKIES Taco Sauce & Dip

2   tomatoes, peeled and chopped

2   tbsp. chopped onion

1   tsp. lemon juice

1   clove garlic, minced

     Tortilla chips

1. Halve, seed, and peel avocados. Mash avocados well. Stir in Salsa, Taco Sauce, tomatoes, onion, lemon juice, and garlic. Cover and chill. Serve with tortilla chips.

Makes: 16 servings

Dill Dip

1   cup real mayonnaise

1   cup dairy sour cream

1   tbsp. dill weed

1   tbsp. COOKIES Flavor Enhancer

1   tbsp. dried parsley flakes

1   tbsp. dried minced onion

1   tsp. garlic salt

     Vegetable dippers

1. Combine mayonnaise, sour cream, dill weed, Flavor Enhancer, parsley, dried onion, and garlic salt. Cover and chill overnight. Serve with vegetable dippers.

Makes: 16 servings

COOKIES Creamy Cheese-Beef Dip

1   8-oz. pkg. cream cheese, softened

5   tbsp. COOKIES Original Bar-B-Q Sauce

¼   cup crushed pineapple, well drained

2   green onions, chopped

1½   tsp. Dijon-style mustard

½   tsp. garlic salt

½   tsp. COOKIES Flavor Enhancer

¼   cup red or green sweet pepper,
     finely chopped

4   to 5 slices dried beef, chopped fine

1   large sweet pepper, for serving

     Corn chips, crackers, or vegetables

1. Combine cream cheese, Bar-B-Q Sauce, pineapple, green onions, mustard, garlic salt, and Flavor Enhancer in a medium bowl. Stir in chopped pepper and dried beef. Chill for several hours. When ready to serve, put into a large pepper with the membrane and seeds removed. Serve with corn chips, crackers, or vegetables.

Makes: 8 servings

El Paso Dip

2   lbs. ground beef
1   small green sweet pepper, chopped
1   small onion, chopped
1   16-oz. can refried beans
1   lb. Velveeta cheese, cubed
1   cup COOKIES Taco Sauce & Dip
½   cup chopped mushrooms
¼   cup sliced black olives
½   tsp. COOKIES Flavor Enhancer
    Chips

1. Brown ground beef with pepper and onion in a large skillet. Drain fat. Add refried beans, cheese, Taco Sauce, mushrooms, olives, and Flavor Enhancer. Cook, stirring occasionally, until cheese melts. Serve with chips.
Makes: 24 servings

Horseradish Dip

2   cups sour cream
½   cup COOKIES Original Bar-B-Q Sauce
1   envelope onion soup mix
1   tsp. prepared horseradish
½   tsp. COOKIES Wings-N-Things Hot Sauce
    Chips

1. Combine sour cream, Bar-B-Q Sauce, onion soup mix, horseradish, and Wings-N-Things. Cover and chill. Serve with chips.
Makes: 16 servings

Ham & Spinach Dip

1   cup ground ham
1   10-oz. pkg. frozen chopped spinach, thawed
    and well drained
1   cup dairy sour cream
½   cup mayonnaise
⅓   cup COOKIES Taco Sauce & Dip
1   8-oz. pkg. cream cheese, softened
2   green onions, chopped
½   tsp. COOKIES Flavor Enhancer
1   loaf French bread
    Party rye bread or pumpernickel bread,
    thinly sliced

1. Combine all ingredients except the breads. Blend well and refrigerate. Cut top off of the French bread. Hollow out loaf, leaving a 1-inch-thick shell. Toast bread shell in a 400° oven for 5 minutes. Place ham and spinach mixture in toasted shell. Serve with rye or pumpernickel bread.
Makes: 16 to 20 servings

Fiery Peanuts

2   tsp. vegetable oil

1   to 1½ tsp. cayenne pepper

2   cups dry-roasted peanuts

1. Heat oil in a medium skillet over medium heat. Stir in cayenne pepper. Stir in peanuts. Cook about 2 minutes, stirring constantly, until peanuts are evenly coated and hot. Cool slightly.
Makes: 6 servings

To quickly crack open a large amount of nuts in shells, put them in a bag and gently hammer until they are cracked open. Remove nut meats with a pick.

Prairie Party Mix

½   cup COOKIES Original Bar B-Q Sauce

1   tbsp. margarine

2   tsp. chili powder

1   tsp. Worcestershire sauce

½   tsp. garlic powder

8   cups crispy corn and rice cereal

2   cups pretzels

⅔   cup peanuts

1. Mix first 5 ingredients in glass measuring cup. Heat in microwave for 1½ minutes. Mix cereal, pretzels, and peanuts in a large bowl. Add sauce and stir. Spread in a shallow roasting pan. Bake, uncovered, in a 350° oven for 35 minutes, stirring frequently. Cool and serve.
Makes: 10 servings

Snappy Pecans

¾   cup COOKIES Taco Sauce & Dip
2   tbsp. butter
2   cups pecan halves
     Dash COOKIES Flavor Enhancer

1. In a small saucepan, heat Taco Sauce and butter. Coat pecans with warm sauce mixture and spread in a single layer in a shallow pan. Bake, uncovered, in a 250° oven for 1 hour, stirring every 20 minutes. Cool on a paper towel. Sprinkle with Flavor Enhancer.
Makes: 8 servings

Spiced Pecans or Walnuts

1   tbsp. granulated sugar
1   tsp. COOKIES Flavor Enhancer
1   tsp. kosher salt
¼   tsp. ground cinnamon
2   tbsp. water
1   tbsp. unsalted butter
1   tsp. packed brown sugar
2   cups pecans or walnuts

1. In a large bowl, combine granulated sugar, Flavor Enhancer, salt, and cinnamon; set aside.

2. In a small saucepan, combine water, butter, and brown sugar; bring to a boil. Stir in pecans or walnuts until coated and liquid is almost gone. Transfer nuts to the bowl with the spice mix and toss to coat. Put on a cookie sheet and let cool.
Makes: 8 servings

Bar-B-Q Baste

2   cups COOKIES Country Blend Bar-B-Q Sauce

¾   cup beer

½   cup butter or margarine (1 stick)

½   cup honey or molasses

1. In a medium saucepan, combine Bar-B-Q Sauce, beer, butter, and honey or molasses. Heat, stirring occasionally, until butter is melted. Remove as much as needed and use to brush on meat during the last 10 minutes of grilling. Cover and chill the remaining sauce. Reheat before using. Store for up to 1 week in the refrigerator.
Makes: enough to baste 5 to 6 pounds of meat

Pork Chop Marinade

1   cup sweet pickle juice

1   cup COOKIES Original Bar-B-Q Sauce

1. Mix pickle juice and Bar-B-Q Sauce; pour over chops. Cover and chill for 2 to 4 hours. Drain, reserving marinade. Grill chops over indirect heat. Bring reserved marinade to boiling and use to brush on chops during the last 5 minutes of grilling.
Makes: enough marinade for 3 pounds of pork chops

COOKIES Mediterranean Meat Marinade

⅓   cup lemon juice

⅓   cup olive oil

1   tsp. crushed garlic

½   tsp. COOKIES Flavor Enhancer

     COOKIES Bar-B-Q Sauce (your favorite flavor)

1. Combine all the ingredients, except Bar-B-Q Sauce. Pour over meat, making sure it is completely submerged. Cover and refrigerate for at least 4 hours. Drain and broil or grill the meat. Baste with Bar-B-Q Sauce of your choice the last 5 minutes of grilling.
Makes: enough marinade for 1 to 1½ pounds of meat

If you don't have lemon juice, substitute half the amount in vinegar instead.

COOKIES Meat Marinade

2   cups water

1   cup corn oil

½   cup COOKIES Original Bar-B-Q Sauce

1   large onion, coarsely chopped

¼   cup lemon juice

¼   cup cider vinegar

3   tbsp. Worcestershire sauce

2   tbsp. yellow mustard

1   tsp. pepper

½   tsp. COOKIES Flavor Enhancer

     COOKIES Bar-B-Q Sauce (your favorite flavor)

1. Combine all the ingredients, except Bar-B-Q Sauce. Pour over meat, making sure it is completely submerged. Cover and refrigerate for up to 24 hours. Drain and broil or grill the meat. Baste with Bar-B-Q Sauce of your choice during the last 5 minutes of grilling.

Makes: enough marinade for 5 to 6 pounds of meat

Marinade for Chicken

1½   cups COOKIES Taco Sauce & Dip

¼   cup water

3   tbsp. finely chopped green onions

2   tbsp. finely chopped green sweet pepper

1. Combine all ingredients and pour over any type of chicken pieces. Refrigerate overnight. Drain chicken and grill over indirect heat.

Makes: enough marinade for 3 to 4 pounds of meaty chicken pieces

Marinating Sauce

¾   cup COOKIES Original Bar-B-Q Sauce

⅓   cup vegetable oil

3   tbsp. vinegar

1½   tsp. soy sauce

½   tsp. dry mustard

¼   tsp. COOKIES Flavor Enhancer

1. Mix all ingredients and pour over meat; cover and chill for 4 to 8 hours. Drain meat. Save marinade to use as a baste during the first half of indirect grilling.

Makes: enough marinade for 2 pounds of meat

SOUPS
& SALADS

Chapter 2

Hot Chili

1   lb. ground beef

1   onion, diced

1   large green sweet pepper, finely chopped

1   16-oz. can pork and beans

1   15-oz. can kidney beans

1   15-oz. can chili beans

1   lb. cubed cooked roast beef

2   cups V8 Juice

½   cup COOKIES Taco Sauce & Dip

1   hot red pepper, diced

3   bay leaves

1   tbsp. chili powder

2   tbsp. butter

1. Cook ground beef, onion, and green pepper in a kettle or Dutch oven until meat is brown. Add the 3 cans of undrained beans to kettle. Place all remaining ingredients, except butter, in kettle. Simmer for 1 hour on low heat. Remove bay leaves and add butter. Stir butter through chili. Serve immediately.
Makes: 8 to 10 servings

the "SAUCEMAN" says

Melba toast, sour pickles, oyster crackers, bread sticks, relishes, and toasted garlic bread make great accompaniments for chowders and meat soups.

Red Snapper Chili

1   onion, chopped

1   medium green sweet pepper, chopped

2   tbsp. cooking oil

3   cups chicken broth

2   cups COOKIES Taco Sauce & Dip

1   14½-oz. can diced tomatoes

1   lb. red snapper fillets, cubed

1. In a large kettle, cook onion and green pepper in oil. Add broth and Taco Sauce. Heat to boil and simmer for 20 minutes. Stir in tomatoes and cubed fish. Simmer for 10 minutes or until fish flakes easily.
Makes: 4 servings

COOKIES Zesty Chili

2   lbs. ground beef

½   cup chopped onion

2   large cans whole tomatoes

2   cans kidney beans

1   cup COOKIES Taco Sauce & Dip

1   tbsp. chili powder (or to suit your taste)

½   tsp. COOKIES Flavor Enchancer

1. Brown ground beef and onions; drain. Add the rest of the ingredients and simmer for 2 hours.
Makes: 6 to 8 servings

White Chili

1   medium onion, chopped

2   tbsp. minced garlic

2   tbsp. cooking oil

6   cups chicken broth

1   tbsp. COOKIES Flavor Enhancer

1   tsp. dried oregano

1   19-oz. can cannellini beans
    (white kidney beans)

1   4½-oz. can diced green chile peppers

1   cup Monterey Jack cheese, shredded

4   cups diced cooked turkey or chicken
    Chopped cilantro, sliced scallions,
      and shredded cheese

¼   cup COOKIES Premium Salsa

1. Sauté onion and garlic in oil. Add broth, Flavor Enhancer, and oregano; simmer for 5 minutes. Add beans, green chiles, Monterey Jack cheese, and meat. Cook for about 10 minutes more. Put in a bowl; top with cilantro, scallions, shredded cheese, and Salsa.
Makes: 6 to 8 servings

Bar-B-Q Chili

2   lbs. ground beef

1   medium onion, chopped

2   21-oz. cans pork and beans

1   46-oz. can tomato juice

1   cup COOKIES Original Bar-B-Q Sauce

1. Brown ground beef and onion in a Dutch oven; drain. Add pork and beans, tomato juice, and Bar-B-Q Sauce. Simmer for 30 minutes and serve.
Makes: 8 servings

Note: May use 4 cups cooked kidney beans in place of pork and beans.

Ham & Cheese Vegetable Soup

1   can condensed creamy onion soup

1   can condensed cheese soup

1   can chicken broth

1   can mixed vegetables, drained

2   to 3 potatoes, cubed

2   cups cubed ham

1   quart milk
    COOKIES Flavor Enhancer

1. Put all ingredients in a slow cooker. Cook on low-heat setting for 8 to 10 hours.
Makes: 8 servings

the "SAUCEMAN" says

If your soup is too salty, place a raw potato piece in the cooking pot to absorb the salty taste.

Hamburger Barley Soup

½ lb. ground beef
¾ cup chopped onion
8 ounces mushrooms, sliced
2½ cups water
1 14½-oz. can stewed tomatoes
2 medium carrots, sliced
½ cup quick-cooking barley
1 tsp. COOKIES Flavor Enhancer
1 tsp. dried oregano
½ lb. Velveeta cheese, cubed

1. Brown ground beef, drain. Add onion and mushrooms. Stir in remaining ingredients, except cheese. Simmer 20 minutes. Stir in cheese until melted. Do not boil.
Makes: 4 servings

Roast Stew

4 lbs. beef chuck roast, cut into 1-inch cubes
2 tbsp. cooking oil
12 baby red potatoes, halved
2 cups diced onion
1 cup diced carrots
1 cup diced green sweet peppers
½ cup diced celery
2 cups water
2 cups COOKIES Original Bar-B-Q Sauce
1 10¾-oz. can condensed tomato soup
1 tsp. COOKIES Flavor Enhancer
1 tsp. chili powder

1. In a large cooking pan, brown meat in hot oil, one-half at a time; return all meat to pan. Add remaining ingredients; stir gently. Simmer, covered, for 1 hour or until potatoes are fork-tender. Thicken with mixture of flour and water, if needed.

2. Serve with warm bread for dipping.
Makes: 8 to 10 servings

Hearty Beef Stew

1   lb. boneless beef chuck steak
½   tsp. COOKIES Flavor Enhancer
1   14½-oz. can stewed tomatoes
1   cup COOKIES Original Bar-B-Q Sauce
3   medium potatoes, halved
4   carrots, halved

1. Place steak in the bottom of a large casserole dish. Sprinkle with Flavor Enhancer. Bake, covered, in a 350° oven for 30 minutes. Remove from oven; cover with stewed tomatoes and Bar-B-Q Sauce. Place potatoes and carrots over the top. Cover and return to the oven for another hour.
Makes: 3 to 4 servings

the "SAUCEMAN" says

If your soup is too greasy, drop a lettuce leaf in the pot. When the grease has been absorbed, remove the lettuce.

Taco Soup

2   lbs. ground beef
1   large onion, chopped
1   15-oz. can tomato sauce
1   15-oz. can whole kernel corn
1   15-oz. can chili beans
1   jar COOKIES Premium Salsa
1   envelope taco seasoning
     Crushed tortilla chips
     Grated cheese

1. Brown ground beef and onion; drain fat. Add tomato sauce, undrained corn, chili beans, Salsa, and taco seasoning and cook until heated through. Serve with crushed tortilla chips and grated cheese.
Makes: 8 servings

Hearty Bean Soup

2½ cups dried pinto beans, washed and
      soaked overnight

4   cups water

2   14-oz. cans chicken broth

½   cup chopped onion

3   bay leaves

1   lb. ham, cubed

1   18-oz. bottle **COOKIES Original Bar-B-Q Sauce**

1. In a 4-quart Dutch oven, combine beans, water, broth, onion, and bay leaves. Bring to boiling, reduce heat. Simmer, covered, 1 hour. Add ham and Bar-B-Q Sauce. Continue to simmer, uncovered, until thickened and beans are tender, stirring occasionally. When ready to serve, remove bay leaves.

Makes: 8 servings

Wild Rice Soup

½   cup chopped onion

½   cup chopped celery

¼   cup butter

½   cup flour

1   10¾-oz. can condensed cream
      of mushroom soup

6   cups chicken broth

2   cups cooked wild rice

½   tsp. **COOKIES Flavor Enhancer**

½   tsp. dry mustard

½   tsp. curry powder

1   cup half-and-half

1. Cook onion and celery in butter until tender. Add flour. Mix to keep from getting lumpy. Stir in soup and broth. Stir in rice and seasonings. Bring to boiling; reduce heat and simmer 30 minutes. Add half-and-half. Heat through and serve.

Makes: 8 servings

Beer Cheese Soup

3   cups water
1   12-oz. can beer
1   cup chopped celery
1   cup chopped onion
4   chicken bouillon cubes
2½ cups cubed, peeled potatoes
1   cup chopped carrots
2   10¾-oz. cans condensed cream
     of chicken soup
1   cup Velveeta cheese, cubed

1. Combine the water, beer, celery, onion, and bouillon cubes in a large saucepan. Bring to boiling; reduce heat. Simmer, covered, for 20 minutes. Add potatoes and carrots; cook, covered, until tender. Add chicken soup and cheese. Heat until cheese is melted and soup is hot.
Makes: 8 servings

Potato Soup

6   medium potatoes, peeled and sliced
2   medium carrots, diced
6   stalks celery, diced
8   cups water
1   onion, chopped
6   tbsp. butter or margarine
6   tbsp. all-purpose flour
1   tsp. COOKIES Flavor Enhancer
1½ cups milk

1. Cook potatoes, carrots, and celery in water until tender; drain. Reserve liquid and set vegetables aside. In same kettle, sauté onion in butter. Stir in flour and Flavor Enhancer. Add milk, stirring constantly until thickened. Gently stir in cooked vegetables. Add some reserved cooking liquid until soup is of desired consistency.
Makes: 6 servings

Cauliflower Soup

2 tbsp. finely chopped onion

6 tbsp. butter

6 tbsp. all-purpose flour

½ tsp. salt

⅛ tsp. pepper

4 cups milk

   Seasoning packet from a 7¼-oz. pkg.
     macaroni and cheese dinner mix

½ large head cauliflower, cooked
     until tender-crisp

1 to 2 medium potatoes, cooked, chilled,
     and shredded (optional)

1. Cook onion in butter in a large saucepan. Add flour, salt, and pepper. Add 1 cup of the milk and stir until smooth. Add seasoning packet and stir until smooth. Add remaining 3 cups milk; boil 1 minute over medium heat, then add cauliflower and, if desired, potatoes. Heat through.

Makes: 4 to 6 servings

Cheesy Broccoli Soup

1 16-oz. pkg. frozen chopped broccoli

2 cups chicken broth

2 cups half-and-half

2 10¾-oz. cans condensed cream
     of potato soup

1 cup Velveeta cheese, diced

1. Combine broccoli and chicken broth in a large saucepan. Bring to boiling; reduce heat. Cook, covered, for 8 minutes. Stir in half-and-half and potato soup; add cheese. Cook and stir until cheese is melted.

Makes: 6 servings

Tuna Macaroni Salad

7   oz. shell macaroni
1   7-oz. can tuna, drained
1½ cups chopped celery
½   cup chopped green sweet pepper
½   cup frozen peas, drained
¼   cup pimiento, chopped
1   tbsp. chopped onion
1   cup salad dressing or mayonnaise
    COOKIES Flavor Enhancer to taste

1. Cook macaroni according to package directions; drain and rinse. Combine remaining ingredients and mix with macaroni. Chill and serve.
Makes: 4 servings

Shrimply Avocado Salad

2   lbs. avocados
1   tbsp. lemon juice
¼   tsp. COOKIES Flavor Enhancer
1   cup diced cooked shrimp
½   cup diced celery
1   small onion, chopped
½   cup COOKIES Taco Sauce & Dip

1. Cut avocados in half lengthwise. Remove seeds; sprinkle halves with lemon juice and Flavor Enhancer. Combine remaining ingredients. Fill centers of avocados and serve.
Makes: 2 to 4 servings

Shrimp Salad

1	lb. shell macaroni
4	hard-cooked eggs, diced
1	medium cucumber, diced
1	large tomato, diced
1	medium onion, diced
3	stalks celery, diced
1	4-oz. can shrimp, drained
	COOKIES Flavor Enhancer
1½	cups mayonnaise
2	tbsp. lemon juice
2	tsp. sugar
1	tsp. yellow mustard
	Milk

1. Cook macaroni according to package directions; drain and rinse. Mix eggs, cucumber, tomato, onion, and celery. Add shrimp. Season with Flavor Enhancer to taste. Mix mayonnaise, lemon juice, sugar, and mustard. Pour over salad. Toss. Add milk to desired consistency. Cover and chill.
Makes: 6 servings

Sea Salad

7	oz. uncooked shell macaroni
1	7-oz. can tuna, drained and flaked
½	cup diced green sweet pepper
¼	cup red onion rings
1	tomato, sliced
1	cucumber, sliced
½	cup olives, sliced
½	cup Italian dressing
1	tsp. COOKIES Flavor Enhancer

1. Prepare shells according to package directions; drain and rinse. Combine remaining ingredients with shells and mix well. Chill. Toss before serving.
Makes: 4 servings

the "SAUCEMAN" says

The waxy preservative on cucumbers is harmless—it can easily be scrubbed or peeled off.

Chicken & Shells Salad

1   lb. shell macaroni (4 cups)
3   cups chopped cooked chicken
1   cup sliced celery
1   cup sliced radishes
1   cup chopped green sweet pepper
¼   cup finely chopped onion
½   cup bottled blue cheese salad dressing
½   cup dairy sour cream
1   tsp. dried tarragon
1   tsp. COOKIES Flavor Enhancer

1. Prepare macaroni according to package directions; drain and rinse. Combine macaroni, chicken, celery, radishes, green pepper, and onion. Blend blue cheese dressing, sour cream, tarragon, and Flavor Enhancer. Stir dressing into salad mixture. Cover and chill.
Makes: 8 to 10 servings

Spicy Chicken Salad

2   cups diced cooked chicken
1   cup diced cooked ham
½   cup diced celery
½   cup mayonnaise
½   cup COOKIES Taco Sauce & Dip
3   tbsp. minced onion
    Lettuce leaves

1. Combine all ingredients and chill for at least 2 hours. Serve on lettuce leaves.
Makes: 3 to 4 servings

Bacon-Broccoli Salad

1	large bunch broccoli
2	cups cauliflower
1	cup raisins
¼	cup chopped red onion
10	strips bacon, crisp-cooked and crumbled
1	cup sunflower seeds
½	cup light mayonnaise
½	cup dairy sour cream
¼	cup sugar
1	tbsp. vinegar

1. Wash and cut up broccoli and cauliflower. Place in a large bowl. Add raisins, onion, bacon, and sunflower seeds. Combine mayonnaise, sour cream, sugar, and vinegar. Add to vegetables and mix well. Refrigerate.
Makes: 8 to 10 servings

Make delicious croutons for soup or salad by saving toast, cutting it into cubes, and sautéing them in garlic butter.

Cauliflower-Broccoli Salad

1	head cauliflower
1	large bunch broccoli
1	cup chopped celery
1	cup raisins
½	cup nuts, chopped
1½	cups salad dressing or mayonnaise
¾	cup sugar
6	tbsp. vinegar

1. Cut florets off the cauliflower and broccoli. Add celery, raisins, and nuts. Mix salad dressing, sugar, and vinegar. Pour over vegetable mixture. Stir and chill.
Makes: 10 servings

Corned Beef Salad

2	cups elbow macaroni
1	12-oz. can corned beef
½	cup sweet pickle relish
2	hard-cooked eggs, chopped
1	2-oz. jar chopped pimiento, drained
½	tsp. **COOKIES Flavor Enhancer**
½	to ⅔ cup Miracle Whip
	Lettuce leaves

1. Cook macaroni according to package directions; drain and rinse. Drain and chop corned beef. In a large bowl, combine macaroni, chopped corned beef, relish, eggs, pimiento, Flavor Enhancer, and enough Miracle Whip to moisten. Serve on lettuce leaves.
Makes: 4 to 5 servings

Taco Salad

1½	lbs. ground beef
1	cup **COOKIES Taco Sauce & Dip**
1	15½-oz. can red beans
1	small red onion, minced
2	8-oz. pkgs. shredded sharp cheddar cheese
1	head lettuce, shredded
4	tomatoes, diced
1	bag tortilla chips

1. Brown and drain ground beef. Add Taco Sauce and mix well. Add beans, onion, cheese, lettuce, and tomatoes; toss lightly. When ready to serve, crush chips and mix with the rest of the salad.
Makes: 6 to 8 servings

the "SAUCEMAN" says

Fresh tomatoes keep longer if stored in the refrigerator with stems down.

Honey Pasta Salad

8   oz. bow-tie pasta (4 cups)

1   large nectarine, chopped

1   cup seedless grapes

½   cup golden raisins

½   of an 8-oz. pkg. cream cheese, softened

¼   cup vanilla yogurt

¼   cup chopped pecans, toasted

2   tbsp. whipping cream

2   tbsp. frozen orange juice concentrate

2   tbsp. honey

½   tsp. shredded lemon peel

¼   cup blueberries

¼   cup raspberries

1. Cook pasta according to package directions; rinse, drain, and cool. Add nectarine, grapes, and raisins. Combine cream cheese, yogurt, pecans, whipping cream, orange juice concentrate, honey, and lemon peel; stir into pasta mixture. Carefully fold in blueberries and raspberries. Chill and serve.

Makes: 8 to 10 servings

Warm Layered Taco Salad

1½   lbs. ground beef

1   cup chopped green sweet pepper

½   cup chopped onion

1   15-oz. can chili beans with chili gravy

1   10-oz. can enchilada sauce

1   8-oz. can tomato sauce

1   cup COOKIES Taco Sauce & Dip

1   10-oz. bag corn chips

1   cup shredded mozzarella cheese

4   cups shredded lettuce

2   cups chopped tomatoes

1. Brown ground beef with pepper and onion. Add chili beans and cook until hot. In a large microwave-safe glass bowl, mix enchilada sauce, tomato sauce, and Taco Sauce. Microwave on 100% power (high) for 4 minutes. In a large salad bowl, layer corn chips, meat mixture, cheese, lettuce, and tomatoes. Pour sauce mixture over everything and toss lightly.

Makes: 6 servings

Corn Slaw

2 cups fresh cooked corn

1 cup chopped green sweet peppers

1 cup chopped carrots

½ cup chopped onion

¼ cup mayonnaise

¼ cup sour cream

2 tsp. vinegar

1 tsp. sugar

1 tsp. yellow mustard

¼ tsp. COOKIES Flavor Enhancer

1. Toss vegetables together. Combine remaining ingredients; stir into vegetables. Cover and refrigerate for several hours.
Makes: 6 servings

Surprise Salad

2 cups water

2 cups instant white rice

1 cup diced green sweet pepper

1 cup diced red sweet pepper

½ cup diced tomatoes

¼ cup diced onion

¼ cup seeded and diced jalapeño pepper

1½ cups COOKIES Taco Sauce & Dip

Lettuce leaves

1. Bring water to a boil. Add rice; cover and let stand for 5 minutes. Fluff rice and add remaining ingredients. Stir lightly. Chill. Serve on lettuce leaves.
Makes: 4 servings

Each guest should eat between ⅓ and ½ cup of a salad side dish, so plan accordingly.

Tomato Salad

1   14½-oz. can stewed tomatoes
¼   cup water
2   3-oz. pkgs. lemon-flavored gelatin
1   cup diced celery
1   cup diced seeded cucumber
½   cup diced green sweet pepper
¼   cup minced onion
¾   cup COOKIES Taco Sauce & Dip
¾   cup mayonnaise
½   cup dairy sour cream

1. Heat tomatoes and water to boiling in a medium saucepan, breaking up any large pieces. Stir in gelatin until dissolved. Add celery, cucumber, green pepper, and onion; mix well. Stir in Taco Sauce, mayonnaise, and sour cream. Put in a 2-quart mold or a 3-quart rectangular baking dish. Chill until firm.
Makes: 8 servings

Vegetable Salad, Mexican-Style

1   12-oz. pkg. dried tri-colored rotini
1   green sweet pepper, diced
1   red sweet pepper, diced
1   cup fresh mushrooms, sliced
½   cup diced celery
1   tomato, diced
½   cup pitted ripe olives, sliced
½   cup pitted green olives, sliced
1   18-oz. bottle COOKIES Taco Sauce & Dip

1. Cook rotini according to package directions; drain and rinse. Place in a large bowl. Add vegetables; mix well. Pour on Taco Sauce; mix well to coat rotini and vegetables. Cover and chill for 2 to 24 hours.
Makes: 8 servings

Cabbage Noodle Slaw

1   16-oz. pkg. medium egg noodles

6   cups finely shredded cabbage

1   cup thinly sliced celery

1   cup thinly sliced cucumber

1   cup shredded cheddar cheese

1   cup plain yogurt

¼   cup salad oil

2   tbsp. white vinegar

2   tsp. sugar

2   tsp. COOKIES Flavor Enhancer

½   tsp. dry mustard

¼   tsp. white pepper

    Paprika

1. Prepare noodles according to package directions; drain and rinse. Combine noodles, cabbage, celery, cucumber, and cheese in a large bowl. Blend yogurt, oil, vinegar, sugar, Flavor Enhancer, mustard, and pepper. Gently toss with noodle mixture. Cover and chill. Sprinkle generously with paprika.
Makes: 14 to 16 servings

Rotini Salsa Salad

¾   cup rotini

½   cup COOKIES Premium Salsa

⅓   cup fat-free mayonnaise

1   tsp. dried parsley flakes

¼   tsp. minced garlic

½   cup frozen whole kernel corn, thawed

1. Cook rotini according to package directions; drain and rinse. Combine Salsa, mayonnaise, parsley, and garlic. Add corn and rotini. Mix gently to combine. Cover and chill for 2 to 24 hours.
Makes: 2 to 3 servings

Potato Salad

6   medium boiled potatoes, cubed

4   hard-cooked eggs, diced

1   cup finely chopped celery

½   cup finely chopped onion

1½ cups mayonnaise or salad dressing

1   tbsp. white vinegar

1   tbsp. yellow mustard

1   tsp. **COOKIES** Flavor Enhancer
    Paprika (optional)

1. In a large bowl, combine potatoes and eggs. Add celery and onion. Mix mayonnaise, vinegar, mustard, and Flavor Enhancer. Pour over potato mixture and stir to combine. If desired, sprinkle with paprika. Cover and chill for 6 to 24 hours.
Makes: 10 servings

the "SAUCEMAN" says

Potato salad is best when made from potatoes cooked in their jackets, peeled, and marinated while still warm.

Sweetened Macaroni Salad

1   16-oz. pkg. rotini

1   14-oz. can sweetened condensed milk

1   cup chopped red and/or
    green sweet peppers

1   cup shredded carrots

1   small onion, chopped

1   cup mayonnaise

½   cup sugar

¼   cup vinegar
    COOKIES Flavor Enhancer

1. Cook rotini according to package directions; drain and rinse. Combine sweetened condensed milk, peppers, carrots, onion, mayonnaise, sugar, and vinegar. Stir in rotini. Season to taste with Flavor Enhancer. Cover and chill before serving.
Makes: 10 to 12 servings

Note: Best if made the night before.

Gazpacho Rice Salad

1½   cups water
1   8-oz. can tomato sauce
1   cup uncooked rice
1   tsp. salt
1   cup diced cucumber
½   cup diced green sweet pepper
1   4-oz. jar diced pimientos
⅓   cup sliced green onions
¼   cup oil
¼   cup red wine vinegar
1   clove garlic, crushed
½   tsp. COOKIES Wings-N-Things Hot Sauce

1. In saucepan, heat water and tomato sauce to a boil. Stir in rice and ½ teaspoon of the salt. Simmer, covered, for 20 minutes. Remove from heat. Let stand for 5 minutes or until liquid is absorbed. Spoon into a bowl. Chill for 1 hour. Stir in cucumber, green pepper, pimientos, and onions. In another bowl, stir together oil, vinegar, garlic, Wings-N-Things, and remaining ½ teaspoon salt. Pour over rice mixture, tossing to coat well. Cover and chill for 2 hours.
Makes: 8 servings

Macaroni Salad

6   oz. shell macaroni
1½   cups cubed cooked ham
½   cup COOKIES Original Bar-B-Q Sauce
½   cup minced celery
¼   cup chopped sweet pickle
3   tbsp. minced onion

1. Cook macaroni according to package directions; drain and rinse. Add the rest of the ingredients. Mix well. Serve warm or chilled.
Makes: 4 servings

Dilled Macaroni Salad

1 lb. elbow macaroni

2 cups chopped cucumber

2 tbsp. chopped green onion

½ cup mayonnaise

½ cup dairy sour cream

2 tbsp. fresh dill, chopped

1 tbsp. lemon juice

COOKIES Flavor Enhancer

1. Cook macaroni according to package directions; drain and rinse. In a large bowl, combine macaroni, cucumber, and onion. For dressing, stir together remaining ingredients. Toss dressing with macaroni. Cover and chill for 4 to 8 hours.
Makes: 10 to 12 servings

Potluck Pasta Salad

20 cups cooked Reames frozen rotini

3 cups chopped celery

3 cups diced tomatoes

2 cups diced or shredded carrots

½ cup chopped radishes

4 cups COOKIES Taco Sauce & Dip

1. Combine rotini and the rest of the ingredients. Let stand for at least 1 hour before serving or refrigerate overnight.
Makes: 40 servings

the "SAUCEMAN" says

To peel a tomato easily, spear it with a kitchen fork and plunge it into boiling water for 30 seconds. The skin will slide right off.

Avocado Salad Surprise

3   large avocados
1   8-oz. pkg. cream cheese, softened
½   cup COOKIES Taco Sauce & Dip
1   cup chopped pitted ripe olives
½   cup chopped walnuts
1   head lettuce, shredded
½   tsp. paprika

1. Peel, cut in half, and pit avocados. Mix cream cheese, Taco Sauce, olives, and walnuts. Spoon into avocado halves. Place on a bed of lettuce. Sprinkle paprika over filled avocado halves and serve.
Makes: 6 servings

Taco Aspic

2   envelopes unflavored gelatin
1½   cups water
1   cup tomato juice
1   bay leaf
1   cup COOKIES Taco Sauce & Dip
½   tsp. salt
½   tsp. sugar
2   lettuce leaves
½   cup dairy sour cream

1. In a medium saucepan, sprinkle gelatin over water and tomato juice. Add bay leaf. Let stand for 5 minutes to soften gelatin. Cook over low heat, stirring constantly, about 5 minutes or until gelatin dissolves. Remove from heat and discard bay leaf. Stir in Taco Sauce, salt, and sugar. Pour into a mold. Chill until firm. Unmold onto lettuce leaves and top with sour cream.
Makes: 6 servings

the "SAUCEMAN" says

To core lettuce, smack head stem end down on countertop, then twist core out.

BEEF, VEAL & WILD GAME

Chapter 3

Bar-B-Q Round Steak

3 medium potatoes

1 1½-lb. boneless round steak, ¾ inch thick

½ tsp. COOKIES Flavor Enhancer

1 cup COOKIES Original Bar-B-Q Sauce

1. Cook and mash potatoes. Spread the potatoes over the uncooked round steak. Sprinkle with Flavor Enhancer. Roll up the round steak and potatoes and tie with kitchen string. Place in a shallow roasting pan. Bake, covered, in a 375° oven for 20 minutes. Top with Bar-B-Q Sauce. Return to oven and bake 40 to 50 minutes more or until tender.

Makes: 6 servings

the "SAUCEMAN" says

Add a small amount of hot, not boiling, milk to mashed potatoes to make them light and fluffy.

Beef Zappers

1 lb. sirloin steak

1 tbsp. cooking oil

1 cup COOKIES Premium Salsa

4 lettuce leaves

4 French-style rolls, split

⅓ cup shredded cheddar cheese

1. Cut steak into thin bite-size strips. In a large skillet, heat oil over medium heat. Add beef and cook until browned. Reduce heat and add Salsa. Heat through. Place a lettuce leaf on bottom half of each roll. Top with beef and sauce, cheese, and roll tops.

Makes: 4 servings

Farmers Steak

2 lbs. boneless round steak, cut 1 inch thick
¾ cup all-purpose flour
1 tbsp. COOKIES Flavor Enhancer
2 tbsp. cooking oil
1 10¾-oz. can chicken gumbo soup
1 10¾-oz. can onion soup

1. Cut round steak into eight serving-size pieces. Mix flour and Flavor Enhancer in a plastic bag. Coat round steak with flour mixture. Heat oil in a large skillet. Brown steak, one-half at a time, in the hot oil. Transfer to a 3-quart rectangular baking dish. Combine soups and spoon over meat. Bake, covered, in a 300° oven for 1½ to 2 hours or until tender.
Makes: 8 servings

Flank Steak

1 1½-lb. flank steak
2 tbsp. vegetable oil
2 tsp. lemon juice
½ tsp. garlic powder
¼ tsp. COOKIES Flavor Enhancer

1. Tenderize flank steak with meat mallet. Mix the oil, lemon juice, garlic powder, and Flavor Enhancer. Brush oil mixture on both sides of the steak. Grill steak directly over medium coals for 17 to 21 minutes (160°), turning once.
Makes: 6 servings

London Broil

1 1½- to 1¾-lb. beef flank steak
⅓ cup lemon juice
⅓ cup oil
1 tbsp. COOKIES Flavor Enhancer
1 tbsp. garlic salt
⅛ tsp. dried oregano, crushed
   Dash coarsely ground pepper

1. Trim fat from steak; score steak on both sides by making shallow cuts in a diamond pattern. Combine remaining ingredients in a large resealable plastic bag set in a shallow dish; add meat. Seal bag and refrigerate for 8 to 24 hours, turning occasionally.

2. Drain steak. Grill directly over medium coals for 17 to 21 minutes (160°), turning once. Thinly slice across the grain to serve.
Makes: 6 servings

Get more juice from a dried-up lemon by heating it for five minutes in boiling water before squeezing.

Mexican Pot Roast

1 3½-lb. beef chuck roast
1 15-oz. can pinto beans
1½ cups COOKIES Taco Sauce & Dip
½ cup chopped onion
½ tsp. COOKIES Flavor Enhancer
   Hot cooked rice
   Crusty bread

1. Place meat in a 4- to 5½-quart slow cooker. Add pinto beans, Taco Sauce, onion, and Flavor Enhancer. Cook, covered, on low-heat setting for 8 to 10 hours. Serve with rice and hot bread.
Makes: 8 servings

Roast Beef á la COOKIES

1   3-lb. boneless beef chuck roast
½   cup beer
1   onion, sliced
1   green sweet pepper, sliced
2   cups COOKIES Original Bar-B-Q Sauce
8   to 10 buns, split and toasted

1. Slice roast into ¼-inch strips and lay in a shallow roasting pan. Add ½ inch water. Bake, covered, in a 350° oven for 1½ hours Remove from oven and carefully drain. Add the beer. Layer rings of onion and green pepper on top. Pour Bar-B-Q Sauce over top. Reduce oven temperature to 300°. Return meat to oven and bake, covered, for 1½ hours. Serve open-face on toasted buns.
Makes: 8 to 10 servings

Whiskey Steak

2   beef ribeye or tenderloin steaks,
       cut 1 inch thick
2   tbsp. butter or margarine
       COOKIES Flavor Enhancer
1   small red onion, sliced
3   tbsp. orange juice
1   tbsp. Worcestershire sauce
1   tbsp. Dijon-style mustard
½   tsp. finely shredded orange peel
3   tbsp. whiskey

1. Flatten steaks with heel of hand or heavy spatula. (Do not pound with a tenderizing mallet.) Heat butter in a medium skillet. Season steaks with Flavor Enhancer. Brown steaks quickly on both sides. Remove and keep warm. Add onion, orange juice, Worcestershire sauce, mustard, and orange peel to pan. Cook and stir until blended. Return steaks to pan and cook for 2 minutes on each side. Transfer steaks to serving plates. Remove skillet from heat and add whiskey to pan. Heat and spoon over steaks.
Makes: 2 servings

Shredded Beef

1   3-lb. boneless beef chuck roast
2   tsp. COOKIES Flavor Enhancer
1½   cups water
1   onion, chopped
½   cup chopped celery
⅓   cup chopped green sweet pepper (optional)
1   18-oz. bottle COOKIES Original Bar-B-Q Sauce
     Buns or hot cooked rice

1. Cut beef roast to fit in a 4- or 4½-quart slow cooker; place in cooker and sprinkle with Flavor Enhancer. Add water. Cook, covered, on low-heat setting for 10 to 12 hours. Remove meat from cooker; discard juices. Using two forks, pull meat apart into shreds.

2. Return beef to cooker. Add onion, celery, and, if desired, green pepper. Add Bar-B-Q Sauce; cook for 3 hours on low-heat setting. Serve on buns or a bed of rice.
Makes: 8 to 10 servings

Swiss Steak in Foil

2   lbs. boneless beef round steak,
        cut into 1-inch-thick slices
1   cup COOKIES Original Bar-B-Q Sauce
¼   cup all-purpose flour
½   tsp. COOKIES Flavor Enhancer
2   tbsp. lemon juice
1   onion, sliced

1. Place steak slices in center of a 24×18-inch piece of heavy duty foil. Combine Bar-B-Q Sauce, flour, and Flavor Enhancer; spoon on top of steak. Sprinkle with lemon juice and layer on slices of onion. Seal tightly. Place in a shallow roasting pan. Bake in a 350° oven for 2½ hours. (Or to grill, use a double thickness of heavy duty foil and omit pan. Arrange medium-hot coals around a drip pan. Place foil packet over drip pan. Grill, covered, for 2 to 2½ hours.)
Makes: 6 servings

Taco Pot Roast

1   3-lb. boneless chuck roast

2   tbsp. cooking oil

2   cups COOKIES Taco Sauce & Dip

1   cup water

1   onion, sliced

1. Brown roast on all sides in hot oil in a Dutch oven; drain fat. Mix Taco Sauce and water. Pour mixture over browned roast. Place onion slices on top of roast. Bring to boiling; reduce heat. Simmer, covered, for 3 hours or until meat is tender.
Makes: 6 to 8 servings

Tenderloin Steaks

6   strips bacon

6   5-oz. beef tenderloin steaks, cut 1 inch thick

¼   tsp. COOKIES Flavor Enhancer

1   cup COOKIES Original Bar-B-Q Sauce

4   tbsp. chopped fresh parsley

1. Partially cook bacon strips; drain on paper towels. Wrap a strip of bacon around each steak. Secure with a toothpick. Sprinkle with Flavor Enhancer. Grill directly over medium coals for 11 to 15 minutes for medium rare (145°) or 14 to 18 minutes for medium (160°), turning once and brushing generously with Bar-B-Q Sauce during the last 2 to 3 minutes of grilling. Sprinkle with parsley before serving.
Makes: 6 servings

Steak & Bean Casserole

1 large can pork and beans
1 2-lb. tenderized round steak
3 tbsp. yellow mustard
¼ tsp. COOKIES Flavor Enhancer
1 cup diced onion
1 cup COOKIES Original Bar-B-Q Sauce

1. Pour pork and beans into the bottom of a casserole dish. Place steak on the pork and beans. Spread with mustard and sprinkle with Flavor Enhancer. Cover with onion and Bar-B-Q Sauce. Bake, covered, in a 300° oven for 2 hours.
Makes: 6 servings

Tenderize steaks by simply rubbing them in a mixture of vinegar and oil, then allow them to refrigerate for two hours.

Texas Swiss Steak

2 lbs. round steak, cut into 1-inch cubes
3 tbsp. all-purpose flour
2 tbsp. cooking oil
½ tsp. COOKIES Flavor Enhancer
½ cup diced onion
¼ cup diced celery
¼ cup diced carrots
2 tomatoes, diced
1 4-oz. can chopped green chiles
1½ cups COOKIES Taco Sauce & Dip
½ cup shredded cheddar cheese

1. Coat cubed steak with flour. Heat oil in a Dutch oven; brown meat cubes, half at a time. Drain fat; return all meat to pan. Sprinkle with Flavor Enhancer. Add onion, celery, carrots, tomatoes, green chiles, and Taco Sauce. Bring to boiling. Bake, covered, in a 350° oven for 1½ hours. Sprinkle with cheese before serving.
Makes: 6 servings

COOKIES Country Ribs

10   to 12 hickory wood chunks

4   to 5 lbs. beef or pork ribs

1   tbsp. COOKIES Flavor Enhancer

1   cup COOKIES Original Bar-B-Q Sauce

¼   cup honey

¼   cup lemon juice

1   tbsp. Worcestershire sauce

1   tbsp. soy sauce

1   tbsp. yellow mustard

½   to 1 tsp. garlic powder

1. Soak wood chunks for 1 hour; drain. Sprinkle ribs with Flavor Enhancer. In a smoker, arrange preheated coals, drained wood chunks, and water pan. Place ribs on rack over water pan. Smoke 3 hours.

2. Meanwhile, combine Bar-B-Q Sauce, honey, lemon juice, Worcestershire sauce, soy sauce, mustard, and garlic powder; brush on ribs. Smoke, covered, for 1 hour or until ribs are tender.

Makes: 4 to 6 servings

Texas Beef Brisket Habañero

20   mesquite wood chunks

1   tbsp. COOKIES Flavor Enhancer

1   tbsp. Adolph's mesquite seasoning

1   tsp. garlic powder

¾   tsp. black pepper

2   3½-lb. fresh beef briskets

1   26-oz. bottle COOKIES Western Style
      Bar-B-Q Sauce

    Dash habañero sauce

1. Soak wood chunks for 1 hour; drain. Combine Flavor Enhancer, mesquite seasoning, garlic powder, and pepper; rub into the beef briskets. Wrap in plastic wrap and chill overnight. In a smoker, arrange preheated coals, one-fourth of the wood chunks, and water pan. Smoke, covered, for 6 hours, adding more coals, wood chunks, and water to the smoker as needed. Combine Bar-B-Q Sauce and habañero sauce. Place meat on large sheets of heavy duty foil; add Bar-B-Q Sauce mixture. Wrap meat and seal foil. Smoke 2 hours longer. Slice to serve.

Makes: 12 servings

Beef Stroganoff

1   lb. ground beef or thinly sliced
    sirloin beef strips
½   cup chopped onion
1   clove garlic, minced
2   cups water
1   4-oz. can sliced mushrooms, drained
1   tbsp. Worcestershire sauce
2   tsp. instant beef bouillon granules
    or 2 beef bouillon cubes
1½ tsp. COOKIES Flavor Enhancer
¼   tsp. pepper
3   cups uncooked noodles
1   cup dairy sour cream

1. Cook beef, onion, and garlic in an extra large skillet until meat is browned; drain fat. Stir in water, mushrooms, Worcestershire sauce, bouillon granules, Flavor Enhancer, and pepper. Add uncooked noodles. Bring to boiling; reduce heat. Simmer, covered, 12 to 15 minutes or until noodles are tender. Gradually stir in sour cream. Heat through, but do not boil.
Makes: 4 to 6 servings

Taco Pizza

1   lb. ground beef
1¼   cups COOKIES Taco Sauce & Dip
1   12-inch prepared pizza crust
1   cup shredded cheddar cheese
1   cup shredded mozzarella cheese
½   cup shredded lettuce
1   to 1½ cups crushed corn chips
2   medium tomatoes, diced

1. Brown ground beef in a large skillet; drain fat. Stir in Taco Sauce. Place crust on a pizza pan or baking sheet. Top with meat mixture and cheeses. Bake in a 425° oven for 20 minutes. Top with lettuce, corn chips, and tomatoes.
Makes: 4 to 6 servings

Beany Bar-B-Q Beef

1   cup cubed cooked beef
1   cup COOKIES Original or Western Style
       Bar-B-Q Sauce
1   cup pork and beans
1   cup sauerkraut
8   slices bacon, cooked and crumbled

1. In a medium saucepan, combine beef and Bar-B-Q Sauce. Bring to boiling; reduce heat. Simmer, covered, for 5 minutes. In another pan, combine pork and beans, sauerkraut, and cooked bacon. Simmer, uncovered, for 15 minutes. Put in serving dish and spread meat mixture on top.
Makes: 2 to 3 servings

Taco Loaf

3   eggs, beaten
1   cup cracker crumbs
½   cup finely crushed corn chips
½   cup chopped onion
1½ cups COOKIES Taco Sauce & Dip
1   lb. ground beef
1   cup shredded mozzarella cheese

1. Mix eggs, cracker crumbs, crushed corn chips, onion, and 1 cup of the Taco Sauce. Add ground beef; mix well. Lightly pat mixture into an 8×4×2-inch loaf pan. Bake in a 350° oven for 1 hour. Spread remaining ½ cup Taco Sauce on top; sprinkle with cheese and bake 15 minutes longer. Let stand 10 minutes before serving.
Makes: 4 servings

the "SAUCEMAN" says

To make a less dense meat loaf, beat an egg white and add it after all ingredients have been mixed.

Savory Green Peppers

6   large green sweet peppers
1   lb. ground beef
2   tbsp. chopped onion
1   cup cooked rice
1½ cups COOKIES Original Bar-B-Q Sauce
½   tsp. COOKIES Flavor Enhancer

1. Cut tops from peppers; remove seeds and membranes. Add water to cover peppers and boil for 5 minutes; drain. In a large skillet, cook ground beef and onion until meat is brown; drain fat. Add rice, 1 cup of the Bar-B-Q Sauce, and Flavor Enhancer; heat through. Stuff each pepper with ½ cup meat mixture. Set peppers upright in a 3-quart baking dish; pour remaining ½ cup Bar-B-Q Sauce over peppers. Bake, covered, in a 325° oven for 30 minutes or until heated through.
Makes: 6 servings

Spanish Spaghetti

1½ lbs. ground beef
1   cup COOKIES Taco Sauce & Dip
2   cups cooked spaghetti noodles
1   16-oz. can refried beans
1   6-oz. can pitted ripe olives,
       drained and chopped
2   cups shredded cheddar cheese

1. Brown ground beef in a large skillet; drain fat. Add Taco Sauce and spaghetti noodles; mix well. Spread half of beef mixture in the bottom of a 13×9×2-inch baking pan. Carefully spoon refried beans on top of meat mixture. Spread remaining meat mixture over beans. Sprinkle olives over the top. Bake, covered, in a 350° oven for 30 minutes. Sprinkle cheese over the olives. Return to oven and bake, uncovered, for 10 minutes.
Makes: 6 servings

COOKIES Easy Grilled Sandwich

1½ cups shredded cooked beef

½ cup COOKIES Original Bar-B-Q Sauce

¼ cup mayonnaise

2 tbsp. chopped green onion

1 tbsp. horseradish

Dash COOKIES Flavor Enhancer

2 tbsp. butter, softened

6 slices Texas toast

3 slices cheese (your favorite)

3 slices tomato

1. Heat beef, Bar-B-Q Sauce, mayonnaise, green onion, horseradish, and Flavor Enhancer in a small saucepan. Butter both sides of Texas toast slices. Grill toast in skillet until golden brown. Place cheese slices on 3 of the toast pieces. Place meat mixture on top of cheese. Top with tomato slices and last 3 slices of toast. Serve hot.

Makes: 3 servings

"SAUCEMAN" says

Sunlight doesn't ripen tomatoes, warmth does. Place tomatoes in a warm spot near the stove or dishwasher where they can soak up a little heat.

Sloppy Joe Pizza

1 lb. ground beef

¾ cup frozen corn

¾ cup COOKIES Original Bar-B-Q Sauce

½ cup sliced green onions

½ tsp. COOKIES Flavor Enhancer

1 12-inch Italian bread shell or prepared pizza crust

1½ cups shredded Colby and Monterey Jack cheese

1. In a large skillet, brown ground beef; drain fat. Stir in corn, Bar-B-Q Sauce, green onions, and Flavor Enhancer; heat through. Place bread shell on pizza pan. Top with meat mixture. Sprinkle with cheese. Bake in a 350° oven for 12 to 15 minutes or until cheese is melted.

Makes: 6 servings

Fiesta Kabobs

1   15¼-oz. can pineapple chunks
1½ cups COOKIES Taco Sauce & Dip
1   lb. ground beef
½   lb. ground sausage
2   eggs, beaten
¾   cup fine dry bread crumbs
18 1-inch green pepper chunks
18 small whole onions, peeled

1. Drain pineapple, reserving juice. Combine juice and Taco Sauce. Mix ½ cup of Taco Sauce mixture with ground beef, sausage, eggs, and bread crumbs. Form into 24 meatballs. Place in a large shallow baking dish. Bake, uncovered, in a 400° oven for 15 minutes. Remove from pan; drain fat.

2. Cook green peppers and onions in boiling, lightly salted water for 3 minutes; drain. Alternate 4 meatballs on a skewer with 3 onions, 3 green peppers, and 3 pineapple chunks. Grill directly over medium coals for 8 to 10 minutes, brushing occasionally with Taco Sauce mixture.
Makes: 6 servings

Meat & Potato Cakes

1½ lbs. ground beef
¼   cup COOKIES Original Bar-B-Q Sauce
1   onion, minced
¼   tsp. COOKIES Flavor Enhancer
1   cup hot seasoned mashed potatoes
½   cup shredded cheddar cheese

1. Mix ground beef, Bar-B-Q Sauce, onion, and Flavor Enhancer. Shape into four ¾-inch-thick burgers. Broil 3 to 4 inches from heat for 6 to 7 minutes per side (160°). Top each burger with ¼ cup of the mashed potatoes. Sprinkle each burger with shredded cheese. Place back under the broiler until cheese is melted.
Makes: 4 servings

Fiesta Ranchero Sloppy Joes

2   lbs. lean ground beef

1   medium onion, chopped

1   15-oz. can tomato sauce

1   cup COOKIES Taco Sauce & Dip

1   green sweet pepper, diced

1   cup crushed corn chips or cooked rice

8   hamburger buns, split and toasted

1. Brown ground beef and onion in a large skillet; drain fat. Add tomato sauce, Taco Sauce, green pepper, and corn chips. Bring to boiling; reduce heat. Simmer 20 minutes. Serve on toasted buns.

Makes: 8 servings

Hamburger Krispies

1½   lbs. ground beef

1   cup COOKIES Original Bar-B-Q Sauce

1   egg

1   cup crisp rice cereal

1   small onion, finely chopped

¼   tsp. COOKIES Flavor Enhancer

1. Combine ground beef, ½ cup of the Bar-B-Q Sauce, egg, ½ cup of the cereal, onion, and Flavor Enhancer. Shape into 10 balls. Place in lightly greased muffin cups. Spread remaining ½ cup Bar-B-Q Sauce over the beef balls. Sprinkle remaining ½ cup cereal over Bar-B-Q Sauce. Bake, uncovered, in a 400° oven for 30 minutes.

Makes: 5 servings

the "SAUCEMAN" says

To store, wrap onions individually in foil to keep them from becoming soft or sprouting.

Double Burgers

2   lbs. ground beef

¼   cup COOKIES Original Bar-B-Q Sauce

¼   tsp. COOKIES Flavor Enhancer

4   thin slices tomato

4   thin slices onion

4   slices cheese

4   hamburger buns, split and toasted, if desired

1. Mix ground beef, Bar-B-Q Sauce, and Flavor Enhancer. Divide mixture into 8 portions; on waxed paper, pat each portion into a circle about 4 to 4½ inches in diameter. Top four of the patties with 1 slice each of tomato, onion, and cheese. Top with remaining patties; press edges to seal. Grill directly over medium coals for 14 to 18 minutes, turning once. Serve on hamburger buns.

Makes: 4 large burgers

the "SAUCEMAN" says

When making hamburgers, mix a little flour with the meat and they will stay together better.

Down Home Maid-Rites

2   lbs. lean ground beef

1   onion, finely chopped

1   cup COOKIES Original Bar-B-Q Sauce

½   cup tomato juice

1   tbsp. brown sugar

1   tsp. chili powder (optional)

1   tsp. yellow mustard

1   tsp. vinegar

1   tsp. Worcestershire sauce

½   tsp. COOKIES Flavor Enhancer

8   to 10 hamburger buns

1. In a large skillet, brown ground beef with onion; drain fat. Add Bar-B-Q sauce, tomato juice, brown sugar, chili powder (if desired), mustard, vinegar, Worcestershire sauce, and Flavor Enhancer. Bring to boiling; reduce heat. Simmer, covered, for 30 minutes. Serve on buns.

Makes: 8 to 10 servings

Note: May substitute COOKIES Western Style Bar-B-Q Sauce or COOKIES Country Blend in place of the Original Bar-B-Q Sauce for a delicious twist on your Maid-Rites.

COOKIES Poor Boy Sandwich

1 lb. ground beef

¼ cup chopped onion

½ cup crushed cornflakes or
       soft bread crumbs

½ cup evaporated milk

½ cup COOKIES Original Bar-B-Q Sauce

1 tbsp. Worcestershire sauce

½ tsp. COOKIES Flavor Enhancer

1 11-oz. loaf French bread

½ cup shredded cheddar cheese

1. Brown ground beef and onion in a large skillet; drain fat. Add cornflakes, evaporated milk, Bar-B-Q Sauce, Worcestershire sauce, and Flavor Enhancer. Cut the French bread in half lengthwise. Remove center portion of bread, leaving a ¼- to ½-inch-thick shell. Divide meat mixture between the shells. Place, filled-side-up, on a 15×10×1-inch baking pan. Bake, uncovered, in a 375° oven for 25 minutes. Sprinkle with cheese. Bake for 5 minutes more.
Makes: 4 to 6 servings

COOKIES Wrapped Beef

1 1-lb. loaf frozen bread dough, thawed

1 lb. ground beef

½ cup chopped onion

¼ cup finely chopped green sweet pepper

½ cup chopped fresh mushrooms

1 3½-oz. can chopped pitted ripe olives

1 cup COOKIES Original Bar-B-Q Sauce

1 cup shredded cheddar cheese

1. Roll bread out on a lightly floured surface to a 15×13-inch rectangle. Brown ground beef, onion, and pepper in a large skillet; drain fat. Add mushrooms, olives, and Bar-B-Q Sauce. Mix well. Spread mixture in a 4-inch-wide strip over the length of the dough, stopping 2 inches from the ends. Scatter cheese over the top of the meat mixture. Fold shorter ends of dough in and bring long sides of dough over meat mixture. Pinch edges together to seal. Place, seam side down, in a 15×10×1-inch baking pan. Bake in a 375° oven for 25 minutes or until golden brown. Let set 5 minutes before serving.
Makes: 6 servings

Note: May also use 6 strips of cooked bacon, placed side-to-side, on top of the meat mixture for a great twist on this recipe.

Applesauce Meatballs

2　lbs. ground beef

1　cup fine dry bread crumbs

1　cup applesauce

2　eggs, beaten

½　tsp. COOKIES Flavor Enhancer

1　tbsp. cooking oil

2　cups COOKIES Original Bar-B-Q Sauce

1　cup tomato juice

1　small onion, chopped

1　green sweet pepper, chopped

1. Combine ground beef, bread crumbs, applesauce, eggs, and Flavor Enhancer in a large bowl. Shape into 1½-inch balls. In a large skillet, brown meatballs, half at a time, in hot oil. Transfer to a 3½- to 4-quart slow cooker. Mix Bar-B-Q sauce, tomato juice, onion, and pepper. Pour over meatballs. Cook, covered, on low-heat setting for 8 hours or on high-heat setting for 3 to 4 hours.
Makes: 6 to 8 servings

Barbecued Western Style Meatballs

3　lbs. ground beef

1　cup quick-cooking oatmeal

1　cup cracker crumbs

1　12-oz. can evaporated milk

2　eggs, beaten

½　cup finely chopped onion

2　tsp. COOKIES Flavor Enhancer

2　tsp. chili powder

½　tsp. garlic powder

3　cups COOKIES Western Style Bar-B-Q Sauce

1. Combine all ingredients except Bar-B-Q Sauce. Shape into 1½-inch balls. Place meatballs in a 13×9×2-inch baking pan. Top with Bar-B-Q Sauce. Bake, covered, in a 350° oven for 1 hour. (Or, brown meatballs, one-third at a time, in hot oil in an extra large skillet. Transfer to a 4- to 4½-quart slow cooker. Add Bar-B-Q Sauce. Cook, covered, on low-heat setting for 6 to 8 hours or on high-heat setting for 3 to 4 hours.)
Makes: 10 to 12 servings

Chili Taco Burgers

2   lbs. ground beef
⅔   cup COOKIES Taco Sauce & Dip
½   cup crushed corn chips
¼   cup finely chopped onion
1   egg
2   tbsp. milk
1   tsp. chili powder
8   hamburger buns
8   lettuce leaves
8   slices cheese (your favorite)

1. Mix ground beef, Taco Sauce, corn chips, onion, egg, milk, and chili powder in a large bowl. Shape meat mixture into eight ¾-inch-thick patties. Grill directly over medium coals for 14 to 18 minutes or until meat is done (160°). Serve on buns with lettuce and cheese.
Makes: 8 servings

For hamburgers in a hurry, poke a hole in the center of each patty when shaping. The center will cook quickly, and when they're done, the holes will be gone.

Cooked Dekraut Swissburger

⅓   cup sauerkraut
2   lbs. ground beef
⅔   cup COOKIES Original Bar-B-Q Sauce
¼   lb. Swiss cheese, finely shredded
    COOKIES Original Bar-B-Q Sauce
8   rye buns, split

1. Finely chop the sauerkraut; add ground beef, Bar-B-Q Sauce, and cheese. Shape into eight ¾-inch-thick patties. Grill directly over medium coals for 14 to 18 minutes or until meat is done (160°). Top with a dash of Bar-B-Q Sauce and serve on rye buns.
Makes: 8 servings

Bar-B-Q Enchilada Casserole

1½ lbs. ground beef

1 small onion, chopped

1 10¾-oz. can condensed cream
      of mushroom soup

1 10¾-oz. can condensed cream
      of chicken soup

2 cups COOKIES Original Bar-B-Q Sauce

1 cup milk

½ tsp. garlic powder

½ tsp. ground cumin

2 cups shredded Colby and
      Monterey Jack cheese

12 7-inch flour tortillas, sliced into 4 strips
      Dairy sour cream
      COOKIES Premium Salsa

1. Brown ground beef and onion in a large skillet; drain. Add soups, Bar-B-Q Sauce, milk, garlic powder, cumin, and 1 cup of the cheese. Mix well. In a 13×9×2-inch baking pan, spread one-thrid of the meat mixture. Top with sliced tortillas. Alternate layers of meat sauce and tortillas, ending with meat sauce. Bake, covered, in a 350° oven for 30 minutes. Uncover, top with remaining 1 cup cheese and bake for 20 minutes longer. Serve with sour cream and Salsa.

Makes: 6 servings

Beef Enchiladas

1 lb. ground beef

½ cup chopped onion

2 cups COOKIES Taco Sauce & Dip

1 8-oz. carton dairy sour cream

1 6-oz. can pitted ripe olives,
      drained and sliced

1½ cups shredded cheddar cheese

10 7- to 8-inch flour tortillas

1. Brown ground beef and onion in a large skillet; drain fat. Add ½ cup of the Taco Sauce, sour cream, olives, and 1 cup of the cheddar cheese. Divide mixture evenly among the tortillas. Roll up and put seam-side down in a 3-quart rectangular baking dish. Pour remaining 1½ cups Taco Sauce over tortillas. Sprinkle with remaining ½ cup cheese. Bake, uncovered, in a 350° oven for 20 minutes.

Makes: 5 servings

the "SAUCEMAN" says

Sprinkle salt in the bottom of a frying pan to prevent meat and other food from sticking.

COOKIES Bar-B-Q Lasagna

1   12-oz. pkg. lasagna noodles

1½ lbs. ground beef

¾   cup finely chopped onion

1   28-oz. can stewed tomatoes

2   cups COOKIES Original Bar-B-Q Sauce

2   cups shredded cheddar cheese

1. Cook lasagna noodles according to package directions; drain. Cook ground beef and onion in a large skillet until beef is browned; drain fat. Add tomatoes and COOKIES Bar-B-Q Sauce. Bring to boiling; reduce heat. Simmer, uncovered, for 15 minutes. In a 13×9×2-inch baking pan, layer half of lasagna noodles, half of meat mixture, and half of the cheese. Add another layer of each in the same order. Bake, uncovered, in a 350° oven for 25 to 30 minutes. Let stand 10 minutes before cutting.

Makes: 6 to 8 servings

French-Fried Onion Beef Bake

2   cups elbow macaroni

1   lb. ground beef

1   10¾-oz. can condensed cream
     of mushroom soup

1   14½-oz. can whole tomatoes, cut up

¾   cup shredded cheddar cheese

¼   cup chopped green sweet pepper

¾   tsp. COOKIES Flavor Enhancer

1   2.8-oz. can french-fried onions

1. Prepare macaroni according to package directions; rinse and drain. Brown ground beef in a large skillet; drain fat. Combine macaroni, beef, soup, undrained tomatoes, cheese, green pepper, and Flavor Enhancer. Place half of the macaroni mixture in a 2-quart casserole. Top with half of the french-fried onions. Add remaining macaroni mixture. Bake, covered, at 350° for 30 minutes. Top with remaining onions and bake, uncovered, for 5 minutes.

Makes: 6 servings

Chuck Wagon Salisbury Steak

1   cup crushed cornflakes

1   egg, beaten

½   cup COOKIES Country Blend Bar-B-Q Sauce

1   tsp. COOKIES Flavor Enhancer

1   lb. ground chuck

1. Place crushed cornflakes in a bowl. Add egg, ¼ cup of the Bar-B-Q Sauce, and the Flavor Enhancer; add ground beef. Mix until combined. Shape into four ¾-inch-thick patties. Grill directly over medium coals for 14 to 18 minutes or until meat is done (160°), turning once halfway through grilling and brushing with remaining ¼ cup Bar-B-Q Sauce during the last 5 minutes of grilling.
Makes: 4 servings

Hamburger Hot Dish

5   cups egg noodles

2   lbs. ground beef

1   cup chopped onion

1   15-oz. can whole kernel corn, drained

1   10¾-oz. can condensed cream
     of chicken soup

1   10¾-oz. can condensed cream
     of celery soup

1   8-oz. carton dairy sour cream

½   to 1 tsp. COOKIES Flavor Enhancer

1   2.8-oz. can french-fried onions (optional)

1. Cook noodles according to package directions; rinse and drain. In a 12-inch skillet cook ground beef and onion until meat is brown; drain fat. Stir in corn, soups, sour cream, and Flavor Enhancer. Transfer to a greased 3-quart rectangular baking dish. Bake, uncovered, in a 350° oven for 45 minutes. If desired, top with onions. Bake, uncovered, for 5 minutes more.
Makes: 8 servings

Bar-B-Qued Meat Leaf

2   lbs. ground beef

1   cup quick-cooking oats

1   egg, beaten

½   cup milk

1   onion, finely chopped

½   cup COOKIES Original Bar-B-Q Sauce

½   tsp. COOKIES Flavor Enhancer

1. Combine all ingredients in a large bowl. Lightly pat mixture into a 9×5×3-inch loaf pan. Bake, uncovered, in a 325° oven for 1½ hours (160°). Let stand for 10 minutes before serving.
Makes: 8 servings

the "SAUCEMAN" says

To get a bottle of sluggish ketchup moving, push a drinking straw to the bottom of the bottle and remove. This will admit enough air to start the ketchup flowing.

Captivating Cabbage Balls

6   large cabbage leaves

½   lb. ground beef

½   lb. bulk Italian sausage

1   small onion, finely chopped

1½ cups water

1   6-oz. can tomato paste

½   cup cooked rice

1   cup COOKIES Taco Sauce & Dip

½   cup shredded cheddar cheese

1. Trim veins from cabbage leaves. Immerse leaves in boiling water for 3 minutes or until limp; drain.

2. In a large skillet, cook ground beef, sausage, and onion until meat is brown; drain fat. Stir in water, tomato paste, and rice. Divide meat mixture evenly among the cabbage leaves. Fold in sides and secure with a wooden toothpick. Place rolls in a 2-quart baking dish. Top with Taco Sauce. Bake, covered, in a 350° oven for 45 minutes. Top with cheese; bake, uncovered, for 10 minutes. Remove toothpicks before serving.
Makes: 6 servings

Burrito Pie

2	lbs. ground beef
1	16-oz. can refried beans
1	cup COOKIES Taco Sauce & Dip
1	small onion, finely chopped
4	7- to 8-inch flour tortillas
2	cups shredded cheddar cheese

1. Brown ground beef in a large skillet; drain fat. Add beans, Taco Sauce, and onion. Lightly grease bottom of an 8-inch pie pan. Place a tortilla in the bottom of the pan. Spread one-fourth of meat mixture on top. Sprinkle ½ cup cheese on top. Repeat 4 times. Bake, uncovered, in a 350° oven for 25 minutes.
Makes: 6 servings

Chilling cheese before grating will make the process smoother and faster.

Cabbage Patch Dish

1	lb. lean ground beef
3	large potatoes, peeled and thinly sliced
3	medium carrots, thinly sliced
3	large tomatoes, sliced
1	large onion, sliced
1	stalk celery, chopped
1	small head cabbage, shredded
1	cup COOKIES Taco Sauce & Dip
½	tsp. COOKIES Flavor Enhancer

1. Crumble ground beef in the bottom of a large skillet. Top with potatoes, carrots, tomatoes, onion, and celery. Cover with shredded cabbage. Pour Taco Sauce over the top. Sprinkle with Flavor Enhancer. Cover. Bring to boiling; reduce heat and cook over medium heat for 30 minutes or until all vegetables are tender.
Makes: 6 servings

Beef & Beans

2 lbs. ground beef
1 onion, chopped
1 large can pork and beans
1 cup cooked rice
½ tsp. COOKIES Flavor Enhancer
1 to 1½ cups COOKIES Original Bar-B-Q Sauce
8 to 10 hamburger buns

1. In a large skillet cook ground beef and onion until meat is brown; drain fat. Add pork and beans, rice, Flavor Enhancer, and enough Bar-B-Q Sauce to moisten. Simmer, uncovered, for 15 minutes or until heated through. Serve on buns.
Makes: 8 to 10 servings

Chalupas

2 lbs. ground beef
1 15-oz. can chili beans with chili gravy
½ cup COOKIES Taco Sauce & Dip
6 to 8 cups corn chips
2 tomatoes, diced
1 small onion, diced
½ head lettuce, shredded
1 small green sweet pepper, diced
1 3½-oz. can chopped ripe olives
2 cups shredded cheddar cheese

1. Brown ground beef in a large skillet; drain fat. Add beans and Taco Sauce; mash slightly. Place 1 cup corn chips on each plate. Place scoop of meat mixture on top of chips. Top with tomatoes, onion, lettuce, green pepper, olives, and cheese as desired.
Makes: 6 to 8 servings

Chuck Wagon Casserole

1½ lbs. ground chuck

½ cup chopped onion

1 31-oz. can pork and beans

1½ cups COOKIES Original Bar-B-Q Sauce

½ cup packed brown sugar

2 tbsp. yellow mustard

⅛ tsp. COOKIES Flavor Enhancer

2 cups shredded cheese

Hot biscuits

1. Cook ground chuck and onion in a large skillet; drain fat. Add pork and beans, Bar-B-Q Sauce, brown sugar, mustard, and Flavor Enhancer. Mix well and put into a 2-quart casserole dish. Bake, covered, in a 350° oven for 30 minutes. Sprinkle with cheese. Bake, uncovered, for 20 to 30 minutes or until bubbly. Serve hot over biscuits.

Makes: 6 to 8 servings

Coney Meat Mix

1 lb. ground beef

1 onion, chopped

1½ cups COOKIES Original Bar-B-Q Sauce

1 16-oz. can pork and beans

½ tsp. COOKIES Flavor Enhancer

Hot dogs

Hot dog buns

1. Brown ground beef and onion in a large skillet; drain fat. Add Bar-B-Q Sauce, pork and beans, and Flavor Enhancer. Simmer for 20 minutes, stirring frequently. Serve over heated hot dogs in buns.

Makes: 8 to 10 servings

the "SAUCEMAN" says

Boil hot dogs in sweet pickle juice and a little water for a different taste.

Mexican Goulash

1   lb. ground beef

1   large onion, chopped

3   cups cooked elbow macaroni

1   14½-oz. can diced tomatoes

1   10¾-oz. can condensed tomato soup

1   10¾-oz. can condensed cream
      of mushroom soup

1   cup COOKIES Taco Sauce & Dip

1. Cook ground beef and onion in a large skillet; drain fat. Stir in macaroni, undrained tomatoes, condensed soups, and Taco Sauce. Heat through, stirring occasionally.
Makes: 4 to 6 servings

Mexican Hamburger Helper

1   lb. ground beef

1   small onion, diced

1   clove garlic, minced

3   cups water

8   oz. uncooked wide noodles

½   cup tomato sauce

½   cup COOKIES Taco Sauce & Dip

½   tsp. COOKIES Flavor Enhancer

½   cup shredded cheddar cheese

1. Cook ground beef, onion, and garlic in a large skillet; drain fat. Add water, noodles, tomato sauce, Taco Sauce, and Flavor Enhancer. Bring to boiling; reduce heat. Simmer, covered, for 20 minutes, stirring occasionally. Top with cheese.
Makes: 4 servings

Veal Cutlets

2	cups bread crumbs
¾	tsp. dried oregano, crushed
¾	tsp. dried thyme, crushed
¾	tsp. garlic salt
4	veal cutlets
3	eggs, beaten
¼	cup cooking oil
1	cup COOKIES Taco Sauce & Dip
½	cup shredded Monterey Jack cheese

1. Combine bread crumbs, oregano, thyme, and garlic salt in a shallow bowl. Dip veal cutlets into eggs, then into bread crumb mixture. Brown cutlets on both sides in hot oil. Lay browned cutlets in baking dish. Cover with the Taco Sauce. Sprinkle with cheese. Bake, uncovered, in a 350° oven for 45 minutes.
Makes: 4 servings

the "SAUCEMAN" says

To keep hard cheese fresh, cover with a cloth moistened in vinegar, or grate the cheese and store in a tightly covered jar in the refrigerator.

Veal Lasagna

10	lasagna noodles
1	lb. veal, cut into ½-inch cubes
2	tbsp. cooking oil
1	28-oz. can tomatoes, cut up
1	6-oz. can tomato paste
1	4-oz. can sliced mushrooms
1½	tsp. COOKIES Flavor Enhancer
1	tsp. dried oregano, crushed
3	cups shredded mozzarella cheese
¼	cup grated Parmesan cheese

1. Prepare noodles according to package directions; rinse and drain. In a large skillet, brown veal in hot oil; drain fat. Add undrained tomatoes, tomato paste, mushrooms, Flavor Enhancer, and oregano. Bring to boiling; reduce heat and simmer 20 minutes. Spread a thin layer of meat sauce in bottom of 3-quart rectangular baking dish. Top with layer of noodles, sauce, mozzarella cheese, and Parmesan cheese. Repeat layers, ending with Parmesan cheese. Bake, uncovered, in a 375° oven for 30 to 40 minutes or until heated through. Let stand 10 minutes before cutting.
Makes: 8 servings

Bar-B-Qued Wild Rabbit

1   wild rabbit
1   cup all-purpose flour
1   tsp. COOKIES Flavor Enhancer
2   tbsp. cooking oil
1½   cups COOKIES Original Bar-B-Q Sauce

1. Have rabbit cleaned and cut into serving-size pieces. Mix flour and Flavor Enhancer in a clear plastic bag. Place rabbit pieces in bag to coat with flour mixture. Heat oil in a large skillet. Place coated rabbit pieces in hot oil and brown. Turn to brown other side. Remove pieces and place in a greased roasting pan. Cover with Bar-B-Q Sauce. Bake, covered, in a 325° oven for 2 to 2½ hours or until tender.

Makes: 2 to 4 servings

Ostrich Bar-B-Q Pita

1½   lbs. ostrich drum or stir-fry pieces
1   tsp. COOKIES Flavor Enhancer
1   cup water
2   cups COOKIES Original Bar-B-Q Sauce
1½   cups chopped onion
1½   cups chopped green sweet pepper
1   tsp. dried cilantro, crushed
     Pita breads
     Shredded lettuce, chopped apple,
        chopped tomato, sliced celery, yellow
        mustard, dairy sour cream, shredded
        cheese, wine, and/or vinegar

1. Place ostrich cubes in a 3½-quart slow cooker; season with Flavor Enhancer. Add water. Cook, covered, on low-heat setting for 6 to 8 hours or until very tender; drain. Shred meat with 2 forks. Cover with Bar-B-Q Sauce. Add onion, green pepper, and cilantro. Cook, covered, for 1 hour or until heated through. Spoon into pita pockets. Top with lettuce, apple, tomato, celery, mustard, sour cream, cheese, wine, and/or vinegar.

Makes: 8 to 10 servings

Slow Cooked Venison

2 lbs. venison stew meat
2 tbsp. cooking oil
1 cup chopped onion
½ cup chopped celery
1 tbsp. dried parsley flakes
½ tsp. COOKIES Flavor Enhancer
2 cups COOKIES Original Bar-B-Q Sauce

1. In a large skillet brown venison, half at a time, in hot oil. Transfer to a 3½- to 4-quart slow cooker. Add onion, celery, parsley, and Flavor Enhancer. Pour Bar-B-Q Sauce over the top. Cook, covered, on low-heat setting for 8 to 10 hours.
Makes: 6 servings

Deer Steaks

1½ cups COOKIES Original Bar-B-Q Sauce
1 tsp. COOKIES Flavor Enhancer
4 venison steaks, 1 inch thick

1. Mix Bar-B-Q Sauce and Flavor Enhancer in a resealable plastic bag set in a shallow dish. Add steaks; seal bag. Cover and refrigerate 8 hours or overnight, turning bag occasionally. Drain, discarding marinade. Grill directly over medium coals for 17 to 20 minutes for medium (160°), turning once.
Makes: 4 servings

Bar-B-Q Venison Meatballs

1   egg, slightly beaten
¼   cup milk
½   cup fine dry bread crumbs
½   tsp. COOKIES Flavor Enhancer
1   lb. ground venison
1   tbsp. finely chopped onion
2   tbsp. cooking oil
1¼   cups COOKIES Original Bar-B-Q Sauce
1½   cups pineapple juice
2   tbsp. cornstarch
     Hot cooked rice

1. Combine egg, milk, bread crumbs, and Flavor Enhancer in a large bowl; add venison and onion. Shape into 1-inch balls. Heat oil in an extra large skillet; brown meatballs on all sides. Transfer to a 2-quart baking dish. Meanwhile, in a medium saucepan, combine Bar-B-Q Sauce, pineapple juice, and cornstarch; cook and stir until thickened and bubbly. Pour over meatballs. Bake, covered, in a 350° oven for 1 hour. Serve over rice.
Makes: 4 servings

the "SAUCEMAN" says

Use an ice cream dipper or melon baller to form meatballs.

Salsa Venison Roast

1   2- to 3-lb. venison roast
1   tbsp. cooking oil
1   18-oz. jar COOKIES Premium Salsa
2   to 3 small onions, chopped
2   tbsp. brown sugar
½   cup water
     Carrots, sliced
     Potatoes, cubed

1. Brown roast in hot oil in a large Dutch oven. Add Salsa and onions. Mix brown sugar and water. Pour over roast. Add carrots and potatoes. Bake, covered, in a 350° oven for 2½ hours.
Makes: 6 to 8 servings

Pheasant & Mushroom Sauce

1   2½-lb. pheasant, cut up
1   10¾-oz. can condensed cream
      of chicken soup
1   cup mushrooms, sliced
½   cup apple cider
⅓   cup onion, chopped
1   tbsp. Worcestershire sauce
¼   tsp. COOKIES Flavor Enhancer
1   clove garlic, chopped
     Paprika

1. Place pheasant in a 2-quart rectangular baking dish. Combine soup, mushrooms, cider, onion, Worcestershire sauce, Flavor Enhancer, and garlic; pour over pheasant, reserving a small amount for later. Sprinkle with paprika. Bake, uncovered, in a 350° oven for 1 hour. Spoon additional sauce over pheasant and sprinkle with additional paprika. Bake for 30 to 60 minutes longer or until tender, spooning sauce over pheasant every 15 minutes.
Makes: 2 to 4 servings

the "SAUCEMAN" says

Use an egg slicer for slicing mushrooms and beets as well as eggs.

Smoked Pheasant Breast

6   to 8 apple, pecan, or hickory wood chunks
5   or 6 pheasant breasts
1   16-oz. bottle Italian salad dressing
1½ bottles COOKIES Original Bar-B-Q Sauce
1   cup honey
¼   cup steak sauce
¼   cup butter, melted
1   envelope onion soup mix
1   tbsp. garlic salt
1   tbsp. packed brown sugar

1. At least 1 hour before smoke cooking, soak wood chunks in enough water to cover.

2. Place pheasant breasts in an extra large resealable plastic bag set in a baking dish; pour on dressing. Cover and refrigerate 8 hours or overnight, turning bag occasionally. Drain breasts, discarding dressing. Combine remaining ingredients in a medium saucepan; heat to a boil. Simmer, uncovered, until thick. Cool slightly and generously brush on breasts, reserving any remaining sauce in refrigerator.

3. In a smoker, arrange preheated coals, drained wood chunks, and water pan according to manufacturer's directions. Pour water into pan. Place breasts, bone side down, on rack over water pan. Smoke, covered, for 2½ hours or until tender (170°). Heat any remaining sauce to boiling and serve with pheasant.
Makes: 10 to 12 servings

PORK
& LAMB

Chapter 4

Bar-B-Q Boneless Pork Loin

4   7- to 8-lb. boneless pork top loin roasts
    (double loin, tied)
1   tbsp. Morton's Tender Quick
    Woodchips (optional)
1½ tbsp. COOKIES Flavor Enhancer
1   26-oz. bottle COOKIES Western Style
    Bar-B-Q Sauce

1. Marinate loins overnight in mild Tender Quick solution. If desired, soak hickory, apple, or cherry wood chips in enough water to cover. Take meat out of marinade and season with Flavor Enhancer. Arrange medium coals around a drip pan; sprinkle drained wood chips over coals. Place meat over pan. Grill, covered, for 1½ to 2¼ hours (150°). Remove and brush liberally with Bar-B-Q Sauce; cover and let stand for 15 minutes before slicing (the meat's temperature will rise 10°).
Makes: 40 to 48 servings

Bar-B-Q Pork Steak

1   1-lb. pork shoulder steak, ¾ inch thick
½   tsp. COOKIES Flavor Enhancer
1   cup COOKIES Original Bar-B-Q Sauce
½   cup applesauce

1. Sprinkle pork with Flavor Enhancer. Cover with Bar-B-Q Sauce. Cover and refrigerate overnight. Grill directly over medium-low coals for 8 minutes. Turn and top with applesauce; grill for 6 to 8 minutes more or until done (160°).
Makes: 2 servings

COOKIES Flavor-Enhanced Pork Loin

1 tbsp. COOKIES Flavor Enhancer

1 tbsp. packed brown sugar

1 4- to 5-lb. boneless pork top loin roast (double loin, tied)

½ cup COOKIES Western Style Bar-B-Q Sauce

½ cup COOKIES Original Bar-B-Q Sauce

¼ cup pure maple syrup

1. Mix Flavor Enhancer and brown sugar; sprinkle on pork. Arrange medium coals around a drip pan; place pork over the drip pan. Grill, covered, for 1½ to 2 hours (145°). Meanwhile, mix the two Bar-B-Q Sauces and maple syrup. When pork reaches 145°, brush with some of the Bar-B-Q Sauce mixture. Grill, covered, for 10 minutes more or until internal temperature is 150°. Remove pork from grill; cover with foil and let stand for 15 minutes (the meat's temperature will rise 10°). Slice and serve with Bar-B-Q Sauce mixture.

Makes: 12 to 15 servings

Cranberry-Glazed Pork Loin

1 4- to 5-lb. boneless pork top loin roast (double loin, tied)

1 tsp. COOKIES Flavor Enhancer

½ of a 16-oz. can whole cranberry sauce (1 cup)

¾ cup COOKIES Original Bar-B-Q Sauce

¾ cup apple cider

1 tbsp. cornstarch

2 tbsp. cold water

1. Rub roast with Flavor Enhancer. Arrange medium coals around a drip pan; place pork over the drip pan. Grill, covered, for 1¾ to 2¼ hours (150°). Remove from grill; cover with foil and let stand for 15 minutes (the meat's temperature will rise 10°). Meanwhile, make cranberry glaze by combining cranberry sauce, Bar-B-Q Sauce, and apple cider in a small saucepan. Bring to boiling; reduce heat. Simmer, uncovered, for 10 minutes. Combine cornstarch and water. Stir into simmering sauce. Cook and stir until glaze thickens and boils; cook and stir for 2 minutes more. Spoon over pork.

Makes: 12 to 15 servings

the "SAUCEMAN" says

If you do not have cornstarch, substitute flour—just double the amount.

Dean's Marinated Pork Loin

1   3- to 4-lb. boneless pork top loin roast
    (double loin, tied)

4   tbsp. meat tenderizer

⅓   cup COOKIES Original Bar-B-Q Sauce

¼   cup lime juice

2   tbsp. packed brown sugar

2   tbsp. soy sauce

2   tsp. Worcestershire sauce

1. Place pork in a shallow dish. Sprinkle each side of roast with meat tenderizer. Pierce deeply with meat fork. Combine Bar-B-Q Sauce, lime juice, brown sugar, soy sauce, and Worcestershire sauce for the marinade. Pour over meat. Cover and refrigerate for 1 hour, piercing every 15 minutes. Refrigerate overnight. Turn and pierce pork every 30 minutes for 3 to 4 hours prior to grilling. Drain and save marinade.

2. Arrange medium coals around a drip pan; place pork over the drip pan. Grill, covered, for 1½ to 1¾ hours (150°), brushing marinade on pork occasionally during the first hour. Remove pork from grill; cover with foil and let stand for 15 minutes (the meat's temperature will rise 10°).
Makes: 10 to 15 servings

Loaded Bar-B-Q Pork Loin

1   4-lb. boneless pork top loin roast
    (double loin, tied)

1   cup water

½   oz. Templeton Rye or 120-proof whiskey

3   tbsp. COOKIES Original Bar-B-Q Sauce

2   tbsp. prepared horseradish

2   tbsp. honey mustard

1. Place pork in a plastic bag set in a shallow dish; pour water and rye over roast. Seal bag and refrigerate overnight. Drain pork and wrap in foil.

2. Arrange medium coals around a drip pan; place foil-wrapped meat over drip pan. Grill, covered, for 30 minutes. Carefully remove foil and baste meat with a mixture of Bar-B-Q Sauce, horseradish, and mustard. Continue grilling for 1 to 1½ hours more or until done (150°), brushing occasionally with sauce mixture. Remove pork from grill; cover with foil and let stand for 15 minutes (the meat's temperature will rise 10°).
Makes: 12 to 15 servings

Holiday Loin

1   12-oz. bottle Italian salad dressing
1   cup vegetable oil
1   cup vinegar
1   cup diced onion
¼   cup butter, melted
¼   cup Worcestershire sauce
4   cloves garlic, grated
1   qt. water
1   4-lb. boneless pork top loin roast
    (double loin, tied)
1½ cups COOKIES Original Bar-B-Q Sauce

1. Combine Italian dressing, oil, vinegar, onion, butter, Worcestershire sauce, and garlic in a blender. Purée for 1 minute; stir in water. Place pork loin in a covered dish or resealable plastic bag. Pour mixture over pork. Cover or seal bag; refrigerate for 24 hours. Drain pork.

2. Arrange medium coals around a drip pan; place pork over the drip pan. Grill, covered, for 1½ to 2 hours (150°). Baste with Bar-B-Q Sauce every hour for glaze. Remove pork from grill; cover with foil and let stand for 15 minutes (the meat's temperature will rise 10°).
Makes: 12 servings

Loin & Lobster

3   cups apple wood chips
1   5-lb. boneless pork top loin roast
    (double loin, tied)
1   26-oz. bottle COOKIES Western-Style
    Bar-B-Q Sauce
5   lobster tails
1   26-oz. bottle COOKIES Original Bar-B-Q Sauce

1. Soak wood chips in enough water to cover overnight; drain. Arrange medium coals around a drip pan; sprinkle with drained wood chips; place pork over the drip pan. Grill, uncovered, for 2 to 2¼ hours (150°), basting with Western Bar-B-Q Sauce the last hour. Add lobster to grill over drip pan the last 12 to 14 minutes, basting occasionally with Original Bar-B-Q Sauce.
Makes: 15 servings

the "SAUCEMAN" says

Serve lobster with steamed clams and baked potatoes—they go great together.

Maple Syrup Pork Roast

⅔ cup maple-flavored syrup

3 tbsp. Dijon-style mustard

2 tbsp. vinegar

2 tbsp. soy sauce

½ tsp. COOKIES Flavor Enhancer

1 2- to 3-lb. boneless pork top loin roast
   (single loin)

1 lb. baby carrots

4 to 6 medium potatoes, halved

1. Stir together syrup, mustard, vinegar, soy sauce, and Flavor Enhancer. Pour over pork in a shallow baking pan. Surround roast with carrots and potatoes. Roast in a 350° oven for 1 to 1½ hours (150°). Cover and let stand for 15 minutes (the meat's temperature will rise 10°). Slice meat and serve with vegetables; spoon cooking liquid over meat.

Makes: 4 to 6 servings

the "SAUCEMAN" says

Before measuring syrup, jelly, molasses, honey, or other similar sticky substances, grease the measuring cup.

No-Fuzz Peach Pork

1 3- to 4-lb. pork loin center rib roast
   (backbone loosened)

1 red onion, chopped

1 tbsp. cooking oil

1 18-oz. bottle COOKIES Original Bar-B-Q Sauce

4 fresh peaches, peeled and diced

1 tbsp. anise seeds, roasted and crushed

1. Arrange medium coals around a drip pan; place pork over the drip pan. Grill, covered, for 1¼ to 2 hours (150°). Remove pork from grill; cover with foil and let stand for 15 minutes (the meat's temperature will rise 10°). Meanwhile, in a large skillet sauté onion in hot oil over medium heat until tender. Add Bar-B-Q Sauce, peaches, and anise seeds. Heat to boiling; reduce heat. Simmer, uncovered, 20 minutes. Ladle warm sauce over grilled pork. Slice between bones and serve.

Makes: 8 to 10 servings

Pork Cutlets

4   pork cutlets, desired size

3   tbsp. butter

1   small onion, diced

½   tsp. COOKIES Flavor Enhancer

2   cups COOKIES Country Blend Bar-B-Q Sauce

1. Brown cutlets in melted butter with onion. Place cutlets in baking dish. Sprinkle with Flavor Enhancer. Cover with Bar-B-Q Sauce. Bake, uncovered, in a 350° oven for 1 hour.
Makes: 4 servings

Pork Roast

1   3-lb. boneless pork sirloin roast or top loin roast (single loin)

2   cloves garlic, minced

½   tsp. COOKIES Flavor Enhancer

½   cup COOKIES Original Bar-B-Q Sauce

½   cup apple jelly

1. Rub roast with minced garlic and Flavor Enhancer. Combine Bar-B-Q Sauce and jelly. Arrange medium coals around a drip pan; place roast over drip pan. Grill, covered, for 1½ hours (150°), brushing with Bar-B-Q Sauce mixture every 15 minutes. Remove pork from grill; cover with foil and let stand for 15 minutes (the meat's temperature will rise 10°). (Or, place roast in a shallow roasting pan; pour Bar-B-Q Sauce mixture over roast. Bake, uncovered, in a 275° oven for 3 hours (150°); turn every ½ hour. Cover and let stand as above.)
Makes: 8 servings

Pork Shish Kabobs

3   lbs. pork or beef tenderloin,
      cut into 1½-inch cubes
1   cup COOKIES Original Bar-B-Q Sauce
⅔   cup orange marmalade
½   cup soy sauce
1   onion, chopped fine
1   15¼-oz. can pineapple chunks
1   onion, cut into thin wedges
2   cups small fresh mushrooms
1   green sweet pepper, cubed
      COOKIES Flavor Enhancer, to taste

1. Place meat in a plastic bag set in a bowl. Combine Bar-B-Q Sauce, marmalade, soy sauce, and chopped onion; pour over meat. Seal bag and refrigerate for 4 hours; drain, reserving marinade. Drain pineapple, reserving juice. Alternate pineapple chunks, meat, and vegetables on skewers. Sprinkle with Flavor Enhancer. Baste with reserved marinade and pineapple juice. Grill directly over medium coals for 18 to 20 minutes, brushing once with reserved marinade (discard any remaining marinade), turning occasionally to brown evenly.
Makes: 6 to 8 servings

Power Cookin' Pork Loin

1   5-lb. boneless pork top loin roast
      (double loin, tied)
5   cups zesty Italian salad dressing
¼   cup COOKIES Original Bar-B-Q Sauce
2   tbsp. honey
2   tbsp. Worcestershire sauce
1   tsp. Grey Poupon Country Dijon Mustard

1. Place roast in a very large resealable plastic bag in a shallow baking dish. Pour 4 cups of the salad dressing over pork; seal bag and refrigerate for 3 hours. Drain pork, discarding dressing. Combine remaining 1 cup salad dressing, Bar-B-Q Sauce, honey, Worcestershire sauce, and mustard.

2. Arrange medium coals around a drip pan; place roast over the drip pan. Grill, covered, for 2 to 2¼ hours (150°), brushing with sauce mixture every 20 minutes. Remove meat from grill; cover with foil and let stand for 15 minutes (the meat's temperature will rise 10°).
Makes: 16 to 20 servings

Smoked Pork Tenderloins

4   to 6 apple wood chunks
2   12- to 16-oz. pork tenderloins
1   750-ml. bottle apple wine
2   cups COOKIES Original Bar-B-Q Sauce
1   cup honey
¼   cup steak sauce
¼   cup butter
1   envelope (½ box) onion soup mix
1   tbsp. garlic salt
1   tbsp. brown sugar

1. Soak wood chunks in enough water to cover for 12 to 16 hours or overnight. Place pork tenderloins in a plastic bag set in a shallow dish; pour wine over meat. Seal bag and refrigerate for 12 to 16 hours. In a saucepan, combine remaining ingredients and heat to a boil. Simmer, uncovered, to desired consistency.

2. Drain pork tenderloins, discarding wine. Brush sauce over pork. In a smoker, arrange preheated coals, drained wood chunks, and water pan according to manufacturer's directions. Pour water into pan. Place tenderloins on the grill rack over water pan. Smoke, covered, for 1¾ to 2 hours (160°). Add additional coals and water as needed to maintain temperature and moisture.
Makes: 6 to 8 servings

Soaked Pork Loin

1   3- to 5-lb. boneless pork top loin roast
    (double loin, tied)
½   cup pineapple juice
½   cup rum
½   cup soy sauce
1   tsp. ground ginger
2   cloves garlic, minced
    COOKIES Western Style Bar-B-Q Sauce

1. Day 1: Put roast in a plastic bag set in a shallow dish; pour pineapple juice and rum over pork. Seal bag and refrigerate for 24 hours, turning roast once.

2. Day 2: Drain meat but leave in plastic bag. Combine soy sauce, ginger, and garlic. Pour over meat; seal bag and refrigerate for 24 hours.

3. Day 3: Drain meat, discarding marinade. Arrange medium coals around a drip pan; place meat over the drip pan. Grill, covered, for 1½ to 2¼ hours (150°). Remove meat from grill; cover with foil and let stand for 15 minutes (the meat's temperature will rise 10°). Slice and serve with Bar-B-Q Sauce.
Makes: 12 to 15 servings

the "SAUCEMAN" says

Want a fresh salad with dinner? Lettuce and celery will crisp up fast if you place them in a pan of cold water and add a few sliced potatoes.

Bar-B-Q Pork Fajitas

1   medium onion

1   cup COOKIES Original Bar-B-Q Sauce

3   tbsp. vinegar

2   tbsp. salad oil

1   clove garlic, minced

2   1-lb. pork tenderloins
    Ground cumin

8   8- to 10-inch tortillas, warmed

½   head lettuce, shredded

½   cup COOKIES Taco Sauce & Dip

½   green sweet pepper, sliced in thin strips

½   red sweet pepper, sliced in thin strips
    COOKIES Premium Salsa (optional)

1. Finely chop half the onion; set aside. Coarsely chop remaining onion and place in a small bowl; add Bar-B-Q Sauce, vinegar, oil, and garlic. Place tenderloins in a plastic bag in a shallow baking dish; pour sauce mixture over pork and refrigerate for 1 hour. Drain pork, reserving marinade; sprinkle lightly with cumin.

2. Arrange hot coals around a drip pan; place tenderloins over drip pan. Grill, covered, for 30 to 35 minutes (160°), brushing with reserved marinade during the first 15 minutes of grilling. Cut pork into thin slices. Place slices of pork on warmed tortillas. Top with lettuce, Taco Sauce, finely chopped onion, peppers, and, if desired, Salsa.
Makes: 8 servings

Tenderloin Roll-Ups

2   1-lb. pork tenderloins

1½   cups COOKIES Original Bar-B-Q Sauce

¼   cup finely chopped onion

2   tbsp. soy sauce

½   tsp. dried basil, crushed

3   or 4 slices thinly sliced ham

4   to 6 cheese slices
    (Swiss, mozzarella, or cheddar)

1. Butterfly both pieces of meat by making a lengthwise cut down center of tenderloin, cutting to within ½ inch of the other side. Spread open. Place knife in the "V" of the first cut. Cut horizontally to the cut surface and away from the first cut to within ½ inch of the other side of meat. Repeat on opposite side of "V." Spread these sections open. Place meat between waxed paper. Pound with the flat side of a meat mallet or with a rolling pin to flatten to ½-inch thickness.

2. Mix Bar-B-Q Sauce, onion, soy sauce, and basil. Lay half of the ham and cheese in a single layer over each tenderloin. Spread on sauce. Roll up each tenderloin from a short side. (The juice that squeezes out may be spread over the tenderloins.) Tie in several places with 100-percent-cotton kitchen string. Cover and refrigerate for 1 to 2 hours to marinate.

3. Arrange hot coals around a drip pan; place tenderloins over the drip pan. Grill, covered, for 30 to 35 minutes (160°). Or, place meat on a rack in a shallow roasting pan. Roast in a 425° oven for 25 to 35 minutes or until tender (160°).
Makes: 4 to 6 servings

Bar-B-Qued Pork Chops

1   cup all-purpose flour
1   tsp. COOKIES Flavor Enhancer
4   pork loin or rib chops, ¾ inch thick
3   tbsp. cooking oil
¼   cup finely chopped onion
1   cup COOKIES Original Bar-B-Q Sauce
¼   cup packed brown sugar

1. Place flour and Flavor Enhancer in a plastic bag. Place one pork chop at a time in bag, close, and gently shake to cover. Heat oil in a skillet over medium heat. Place pork chops and onion in skillet and cook until meat is brown, turning once. Combine Bar-B-Q Sauce and brown sugar. Pour over chops. Heat to boiling; reduce heat. Simmer, covered, for 30 minutes or until tender.
Makes: 4 servings

Chinese Pork Chops

2   tbsp. cooking oil
4   pork loin or rib chops, ¾ inch thick
¼   tsp. COOKIES Flavor Enhancer
4   thick slices onion
16   uncooked prunes
2   cups COOKIES Original Bar-B-Q Sauce

1. Heat oil in skillet over medium heat. Sprinkle chops with Flavor Enhancer. Brown chops in hot oil, turning once. Place 1 onion slice and 4 prunes on each chop. Pour Bar-B-Q Sauce over chops. Heat to boiling; reduce heat. Cook, covered, over low heat for 30 minutes or until tender.
Makes: 4 servings

Fruited Pork Chops

6   boneless pork loin chops, ¾ inch thick
    Cooking oil
½   tsp. ground allspice
½   tsp. COOKIES Flavor Enhancer
1   15- or 16-oz. can sliced peaches
½   cup seedless raspberry preserves
¼   cup COOKIES Western Style Bar-B-Q Sauce
1   tbsp. grated orange peel
½   tsp. minced garlic

1. Heat a large skillet over medium heat. Brush chops lightly with oil. Season with allspice and Flavor Enhancer. Brown chops on both sides in hot oil; remove from skillet and keep warm. Add remaining ingredients to the skillet and stir to mix. Heat until mixture starts to bubble. Return chops to skillet; simmer, covered, for 30 minutes or until tender.
Makes: 4 servings

the "SAUCEMAN" says

Before using the pulp of citrus fruits, grate the peel, avoiding the bitter-tasting inner white rind. Place in a tightly covered container and freeze until needed.

German-Style Pork Chops

    Cooking oil
4   6- to 8-oz. pork loin or rib chops,
     ¾ inch thick
    COOKIES Flavor Enhancer
1   32-oz. jar sauerkraut
¼   cup packed brown sugar
¼   tsp. caraway seeds (optional)

1. Lightly coat skillet with oil; heat over medium heat. Brown pork chops on both sides in hot skillet. Season with Flavor Enhancer to taste. Add sauerkraut, brown sugar, and, if desired, caraway seeds. Heat to boiling; reduce heat. Simmer, covered, for 30 minutes or until tender.
Makes: 4 servings

Glazed Grilled Chops

1   cup apricot or peach preserves

¾   cup COOKIES Original Bar-B-Q Sauce

¼   cup light-color corn syrup

2   tbsp. vinegar

1   envelope (½ of a box) dry onion soup mix

¼   tsp. ground cloves

4   pork loin or rib chops, ¾ inch thick

1. For sauce, combine all ingredients except chops. Grill pork chops directly over medium coals for 12 to 14 minutes or until tender (160°), brushing occasionally with sauce.

Makes: 4 servings

Heavenly Pork Chops

2   tbsp. cooking oil

4   pork loin or rib chops, 1 inch thick

1½   cups COOKIES Original Bar-B-Q Sauce

1   7-oz. box Minute Rice, uncooked

1   green sweet pepper, chopped

½   cup chopped onion

1. Heat oil in skillet over medium heat; brown chops on both sides. Place chops in a large baking dish. Combine remaining ingredients; pour over chops. Bake, covered, in a 325° oven for 2½ hours or until rice is cooked and chops are tender.

Makes: 4 servings

Louisiana-Style Pork Chops

6   boneless pork loin or rib chops,
         ¾ inch thick
3   tbsp. butter
1   medium onion, sliced
1   medium green sweet pepper, sliced
1   18-oz. bottle COOKIES Taco Sauce & Dip
3   tbsp. COOKIES Wings-N-Things Hot Sauce

1. In a large skillet, brown pork chops in butter on both sides over medium heat. Remove chops and set aside, reserving drippings in skillet. In same skillet sauté onion and green pepper until tender. Return chops and stir in Taco Sauce and Wings-N-Things. Heat to boiling; reduce heat. Simmer, uncovered, for 30 minutes or until chops are tender.
Makes: 6 servings

Pork Chops à la Orange

1   tbsp. butter
6   boneless pork loin chops, 1 inch thick
1   11-oz. can mandarin oranges
¾   cup COOKIES Original Bar-B-Q Sauce
¼   cup packed brown sugar
3   whole cloves
1   tsp. dry mustard
½   tsp. ground cinnamon

1. Heat butter in a large skillet over medium heat. Brown chops on both sides. Drain oranges, saving juice; set aside. Combine ½ cup of the juice, Bar-B-Q Sauce, brown sugar, cloves, mustard, and cinnamon. Pour over chops. Heat to boiling; reduce heat. Simmer, covered, for 30 minutes or until tender. Place oranges on top of chops the last 5 minutes of cooking time.
Makes: 6 servings

Salsa Pork Chops

4   boneless pork loin chops, ¾ to 1 inch thick

2   tbsp. olive oil

      COOKIES Flavor Enhancer, to taste

4   slices low-fat cheese

4   tbsp. COOKIES Premium Salsa
      (mild or medium)

1. Brush pork chops with olive oil and sprinkle with Flavor Enhancer to taste. Grill chops directly over medium coals for 11 to 13 minutes or until tender (160°). Place cheese slices on top and let melt. Remove from grill and top with Salsa.
Makes: 4 servings

Soda Pop Chops

1   cup COOKIES Original Bar-B-Q Sauce

1   cup soda

8   boneless pork loin chops, ¾ to 1 inch thick

1. Combine Bar-B-Q Sauce and soda in a shallow baking dish. Add the pork chops, spooning Bar-B-Q Sauce mixture over to coat. Bake, uncovered, in a 350° oven for 45 to 60 minutes or until tender.
Makes: 8 servings

Bar-B-Q Pork Meat Loaf

¼   cup finely chopped celery

¼   cup finely chopped onion

1   tbsp. cooking oil

2   eggs, beaten

½   cup milk

1   tsp. COOKIES Flavor Enhancer

½   tsp. dried oregano, crushed

½   tsp. dried sage, crushed

1½ cups soft bread crumbs

1½ lbs. ground pork

½   cup COOKIES Western Style Bar-B-Q Sauce

4   oz. shredded cheddar cheese

1. In a large skillet, cook celery and onion in hot oil for 5 minutes or until tender (not brown). In a large bowl, combine eggs and milk. Stir in Flavor Enhancer, oregano, sage, and celery-onion mixture. Add bread crumbs and ground pork. Shape into a loaf and place in a 9×5×3-inch loaf pan. Brush some Bar-B-Q Sauce on the top. Bake in a 350° oven for 1½ hours. Brush on more Bar-B-Q Sauce about halfway through baking time. Remove from oven and sprinkle with cheese. Let stand until cheese melts.
Makes: 6 to 8 servings

Bar-B-Qued Pork Maid-Rites

2   lbs. ground pork

¼   cup chopped onion

2   cups COOKIES Country Blend Bar-B-Q Sauce

1   tbsp. COOKIES Flavor Enhancer

6   to 8 hamburger buns, split and toasted,
      if desired

1. Brown ground pork with onion; drain fat. Pour on Bar-B-Q Sauce and heat through. Season with Flavor Enhancer. Serve on buns.
Makes: 6 to 8 servings

the "SAUCEMAN" says

Keep herbs and spices on the shelf in alphabetical order so they're easy to find.

COOKIES Skillet Dinner

1½ lbs. bulk pork sausage
¼   cup chopped onion
¼   cup chopped green sweet pepper
¼   cup sliced mushrooms
2   cups uncooked macaroni
1   16-oz. can tomatoes, cut up (undrained)
1½ cups COOKIES Taco Sauce & Dip
¼   tsp. COOKIES Flavor Enhancer

1. In a large skillet, cook sausage, onion, green pepper, and mushrooms until meat is brown and vegetables are tender; drain fat. Add macaroni, tomatoes, Taco Sauce, and Flavor Enhancer. Heat to boiling; reduce heat. Simmer, covered, for 20 minutes or until macaroni is tender.
Makes: 4 to 6 servings

Fiesta Pie

1   lb. mild pork sausage
⅓   cup chopped onion
1   cup COOKIES Premium Salsa
1½ cups Monterey Jack or cheddar
        cheese, shredded
1   cup corn bread mix
3   eggs
1   cup milk
4   to 5 drops COOKIES Wings-N-Things Hot Sauce
        Sliced jalapeño peppers, cherry tomatoes,
        and chopped fresh cilantro

1. Place sausage and onion in a microwave colander and microwave on high for 4 to 6 minutes, stirring once or twice. (Or, brown in a skillet over medium heat.) Drain off fat. Place sausage mixture in a 1-quart casserole. Stir in Salsa; spread evenly and sprinkle with cheese.

2. In a medium bowl, combine corn bread mix, eggs, milk, and Wings-N-Things. Beat until smooth. Pour over sausage mixture and bake in a 400° oven for 25 to 30 minutes until top is brown and a knife inserted in center of topping comes out clean. Garnish with jalapeño peppers, cherry tomatoes, and cilantro. Let stand for 5 to 10 minutes before serving.
Makes: 6 servings

Grilled Pork Patties

2   lbs. ground pork
2   eggs, beaten
1   cup crushed saltine or rich round crackers
½   cup COOKIES Original Bar-B-Q Sauce
⅓   cup diced onion
¼   cup diced green sweet pepper

1. Mix all ingredients. Shape into ¾-inch-thick patties. Grill directly over medium coals for 14 to 18 minutes (160°). (Or, place on unheated rack of broiler pan; broil 3 to 4 inches from heat for 14 to 18 minutes.)
Makes: 6 to 8 servings

Note: These patties taste great with a slice of bacon wrapped around each. Secure bacon with toothpick and cook as desired.

Mexican Hot Dish

1½   lbs. ground pork
1   small onion, chopped
2   tsp. chili powder
½   tsp. paprika
¼   tsp. COOKIES Flavor Enhancer
¼   tsp. dried oregano, crushed
1   16-oz. can Mexican chili beans
14   oz. COOKIES Taco Sauce & Dip
1   8-oz. can tomato sauce
8   oz. Nacho Doritos, crushed
1½   cups shredded cheddar cheese
1   cup dairy sour cream

1. Brown ground pork and onion in a large ovenproof skillet; drain fat. Add chili powder, paprika, Flavor Enhancer, and oregano. Add beans, Taco Sauce, and tomato sauce. Add half of the crushed Doritos and ½ cup of the cheese; mix well. Bake in a 350° oven for 25 minutes. Top with sour cream, remaining crushed Doritos, and remaining 1 cup cheese. Bake for 15 to 20 minutes more or until heated through.
Makes: 4 to 6 servings

the "SAUCEMAN" says

As a rule, don't freeze cheese. Freezing will affect the body and texture of most cheeses. They may be suitable for cooking but will appear crumbly or mealy.

Pasta Wheeled Casserole

1   lb. ground pork

1½ cups uncooked pasta wheels

1¼ cups water

1   10¾-oz. can golden mushroom soup

1   cup shredded cheddar cheese

½ cup chopped celery

½ cup milk

1   tbsp. instant minced onion

½ tsp. COOKIES Flavor Enhancer

1. Cook ground pork in a large skillet; drain fat. Combine with rest of ingredients. Place in a 2-quart casserole dish. Bake, uncovered, in a 350° oven for 30 minutes or until pasta is tender.

Makes: 4 servings

Pineapple Tidbit Bites

1   15-oz. can pineapple tidbits

1   lb. ground pork

1   lb. ground beef

2   slices white bread, crumbled (1½ cups)

1   egg

1   tbsp. diced onion

1½ cups COOKIES Original Bar-B-Q Sauce

1. Drain pineapple and reserve juice. Mix pork, beef, bread crumbs, egg, onion, and 2 tablespoons reserved pineapple juice. Mold meat mixture around each pineapple tidbit. Place in a glass baking dish. Pour Bar-B-Q Sauce over top. Bake in a 350° oven for 30 to 45 minutes.

Makes: 8 servings

Pork & Beef Sandwiches

1½	lbs. beef stew meat, cut into 2-inch cubes
1½	lbs. pork loin, cut into 2-inch cubes
2	cups chopped onion
3	green sweet peppers, chopped
1	26-oz. bottle COOKIES Original Bar-B-Q Sauce
10	to 14 hamburger buns, split and toasted

1. Combine all ingredients except buns in a 3½- to 4-quart slow cooker. Cook, covered, on low-heat setting for 8 to 12 hours. Use a wire whisk to stir meat mixture when done cooking. Stir until all meat is shredded and mixed well. Add ½ cup water if mixture is dry. Cover and continue to cook on low for another hour to completely blend flavors. Serve on buns.
Makes: 10 to 14 servings

Pork Rolls

6	boneless pork shoulder steaks, ½ to ¾ inch thick
1	tsp. COOKIES Flavor Enhancer
1	egg, beaten
¼	cup milk
2	cups cubed bread
½	lb. ground beef
¼	cup diced onion
1	tsp. yellow mustard
2	cups COOKIES Original Bar-B-Q Sauce

1. Trim any fat from pork steaks. Place between sheets of waxed paper and pound flat with a meat mallet. Sprinkle with Flavor Enhancer. In a bowl, combine egg, milk, and bread cubes. Add ground beef, onion, and mustard to egg mixture. Divide beef and egg mixture evenly among pork steaks. Roll up and secure with toothpicks. Place in a single layer in bottom of a lightly greased baking dish. Pour Bar-B-Q Sauce over pork rolls. Bake, uncovered, in a 350° oven for 1½ to 2 hours or until tender.
Makes: 6 servings

Italian Sausage COOKIES-Style

12 Italian sausages

1 cup beer

1 cup chopped green sweet peppers

1 cup chopped onions

   Cooking oil

1 26-oz. bottle COOKIES Country
   Blend Bar-B-Q Sauce

¼ cup molasses

12 hoagie-style buns

1. Pierce sausages with a fork. Place sausages in a large skillet; add beer. Heat to boiling; reduce heat. Simmer, uncovered, for 10 minutes or until done; drain. Arrange sausages in a 13×9×2-inch baking pan. In same skillet cook peppers and onions in hot oil until tender. Add Bar-B-Q Sauce and molasses. Pour over sausages. Bake, uncovered, in a 350° oven for 45 minutes, or until bubbly. Serve on hoagie buns or over pasta.
Makes: 12 servings

Pork with a Twist

4 oz. uncooked corkscrew macaroni

½ cup chopped onion

⅓ cup chopped green sweet pepper

1 tbsp. butter

1 10¾-oz. can condensed cream of celery soup

½ cup COOKIES Original Bar-B-Q Sauce

1 12-oz. can luncheon meat,
   cut into bite-size cubes

⅓ cup shredded cheddar cheese

1. Cook macaroni as directed on package. In a large skillet, cook onion and green pepper in butter until tender. Add soup and Bar-B-Q Sauce; mix well. Carefully stir in cooked macaroni, luncheon meat, and cheese. Pour into an ungreased 1½-quart casserole. Bake, covered, in a 375° oven for 45 minutes.
Makes: 4 servings

Luau Ribs

5   lbs. pork country-style ribs, loin back ribs, or spareribs
1   tsp. COOKIES Flavor Enhancer
2   cups COOKIES Original Bar-B-Q Sauce
2   4½-oz. jars peach baby food
2   tbsp. soy sauce
2   tsp. ground ginger
1   clove garlic, crushed

1. Cut ribs into portions that will fit in rib rack. Rub ribs with Flavor Enhancer. Arrange medium-hot coals around a drip pan; place ribs in a rib rack over drip pan. Grill, covered, for 45 minutes. Meanwhile, mix Bar-B-Q Sauce, baby food, soy sauce, ginger, and garlic. Baste ribs; grill for 45 to 75 minutes more or until tender, basting every 10 minutes. Do not turn during this time.
Makes: 6 to 8 servings

Top ribs with a can of halved peaches with juice for a great twist on any rib recipe.

Mexican Ribs & Rice

4   lbs. pork loin back ribs or spareribs
2   cups COOKIES Taco Sauce & Dip
1½ cups water
1   cup uncooked white rice
1   cup chopped onion
1   small green sweet pepper, chopped
½   cup grated cheddar cheese

1. Cut ribs into serving-size pieces and place in a large Dutch oven. Cover with water. Bring to boiling; turn down to simmer. Cook, covered for 20 to 30 minutes or until tender; drain. Combine Taco Sauce, water, rice, onion, and green pepper; pour over ribs. Heat to boiling; reduce heat. Simmer for 30 minutes longer or until the rice is done. Arrange ribs on platter and place rice in the center. Top with cheese.
Makes: 4 to 6 servings

Cajun Ribs & Rice

4   to 5 lbs. pork country-style ribs
3   cups COOKIES Original Bar-B-Q Sauce
3   tbsp. COOKIES Flavor Enhancer
2   tbsp. chile pepper
1   tbsp. coarse ground pepper
    Dash Wings-N-Things Hot Sauce
3   cups cooked Minute Rice

1. Cut ribs into serving-size pieces and place in a large Dutch oven. Cover with water. Bring to boiling; turn down to simmer. Cook, covered, for 20 to 30 minutes or until tender; drain. Mix Bar-B-Q Sauce, Flavor Enhancer, chile pepper, ground pepper, and Wings-N-Things in a bowl. Arrange medium-hot coals around a drip pan; place ribs in a rib rack over drip pan. Grill, covered, for 30 minutes or until glazed, basting with sauce mixture occasionally. When done, serve on a bed of rice.
Makes: 6 to 8 servings

Country-Style Ribs

4   lbs. pork country-style ribs
3   cups COOKIES Original Bar-B-Q Sauce
¼   cup diced onion
¼   cup honey
1   tsp. COOKIES Flavor Enhancer

1. Cut ribs into serving-size pieces and place in a large Dutch oven. Cover with water. Bring to boiling; turn down to simmer. Cook, covered, for 20 to 30 minutes or until tender; drain. Arrange ribs in a shallow baking pan. Combine Bar-B-Q Sauce, onion, honey, and Flavor Enhancer; pour over ribs. Bake, covered, in a 300° oven for 1 hour or until glazed and heated through, turning once to ensure good coating of Bar-B-Q Sauce.
Makes: 6 servings

COOKIES Surprise Bar-B-Q Ribs

6   lbs. pork or beef ribs

1   12-oz. can beer

COOKIES Original Bar-B-Q Sauce

1. Place ribs in a roasting pan. Add beer. Bake, covered, in a 325° oven until tender. Remove from pan; drain well. Reduce oven temperature to 275°. Place ribs on a flat baking sheet. Cover with Bar-B-Q Sauce. Bake for 30 minutes or until hot.
Makes: 4 to 6 servings

Oven Baked Ribs & Kraut

3   lbs. pork loin back ribs,
        cut into 2-rib portions

1   27-oz. can sauerkraut, drained

4   large potatoes, peeled and sliced

⅓   cup chicken broth

½   tsp. celery seeds

1   medium onion, sliced

½   tsp. COOKIES Flavor Enhancer

1   cup COOKIES Original Bar-B-Q Sauce

1. Place ribs, meaty side down, in a shallow roasting pan. Roast in a 450° oven for 20 minutes. Remove from oven and drain. Reduce oven temperature to 350°. Combine sauerkraut, potatoes, broth, and celery seeds. Place in the bottom of a 13×9×2-inch baking dish. Separate onion into rings. Place on top of the sauerkraut mixture. Place ribs, meaty side up, in center of baking dish. Sprinkle with Flavor Enhancer. Cover with Bar-B-Q Sauce. Bake, covered, for another 2 hours or until vegetables and meat are tender.
Makes: 6 servings

the "SAUCEMAN" says

Small, red, waxy potatoes are hearty. They hold their shape when sliced or diced and do not absorb an excessive amount of dressing or become mushy.

Double-Smoked Ham

4   cups hickory chips
1   6- to 8-lb. bone-in cooked ham with
    natural juices (may be spiral sliced)
1   cup COOKIES Western Style Bar-B-Q Sauce
1   cup COOKIES Original Bar-B-Q Sauce
¼   cup pure maple syrup
3   tbsp. Rose's lime juice
    (may substitute lemon or lime juice)
⅔   cup water
⅓   cup all-purpose flour
    Salt and pepper

1. Soak hickory chips in enough water to cover for at least 1 hour; drain. Set ham, cut side down, in a 13×9×2-inch baking pan. Arrange medium coals around edges of grill; sprinkle drained wood chips over coals. Set pan with ham on the grill rack, not over coals. Grill, covered, for 2 to 2½ hours (140°). Drain off liquid and reserve for delicious ham gravy. Mix Bar-B-Q Sauces, syrup, and lime juice. Pour over ham in the pan and return to the grill. Leave on grill while you are making the ham gravy. Remove from grill. Slice and serve.

2. For gravy, measure pan juices; add water to make 2½ cups. In a medium saucepan, stir ⅔ cup water into flour until smooth; add pan juices. Cook and stir until thickened and bubbly; cook and stir for 1 minute more. Season to taste with salt and pepper.
Makes: 14 to 16 servings

Ham & Cheese Pie

2   cups chopped smoked ham
1   cup shredded Swiss cheese
½   cup chopped mushrooms
⅓   cup diced onion
4   eggs, beaten
2   cups milk
1   cup Bisquick
⅓   cup COOKIES Taco Sauce & Dip
¼   tsp. COOKIES Flavor Enhancer

1. Grease a 10-inch pie plate. Sprinkle ham, cheese, mushrooms, and onion onto plate. Combine eggs, milk, Bisquick, Taco Sauce, and Flavor Enhancer. Beat until smooth; pour over ham mixture. Bake, uncovered, in a 400° oven for 35 to 40 minutes until golden and a toothpick inserted in center comes out clean. Cool for 5 minutes and serve.
Makes: 6 servings

COOKIES Ham Loaf

2   eggs

1   cup milk

1   cup cracker crumbs

2   tbsp. chopped celery

2   tbsp. chopped onion

½   tsp. COOKIES Flavor Enhancer

1   lb. ground ham

½   lb. lean ground beef

    COOKIES Original Bar-B-Q Sauce

1. In a large bowl, combine eggs, milk, cracker crumbs, celery, onion, and Flavor Enhancer. Add ham and ground beef and mix well. Form into four loaves; place in 13×9×2-inch baking pan. Pour Bar-B-Q Sauce over loaves and bake in a 350° oven for 1 hour.
Makes: 4 to 6 servings

French Hunter Dinner

1   lb. cooked ham, cubed

½   lb. bacon, diced

6   oz. cooked spaghetti or 1½ cups
    cooked macaroni or noodles

1   10¾-oz. can condensed cream of celery soup

1   16-oz. can lima beans, drained

1   12-oz. can whole kernel corn, drained

½   cup COOKIES Original Bar-B-Q Sauce

1. Brown and drain ham in a large skillet; transfer to a large bowl and set aside. Brown and drain bacon; add to ham. Add spaghetti, soup, beans, corn, and Bar-B-Q Sauce. Spoon into a 3- to 4-quart casserole. Bake, uncovered, in a 375° oven for 35 to 40 minutes or until heated through. Serve with tossed salad and hot bread for an entire meal.
Makes: 4 to 6 servings

the "SAUCEMAN" says

Great sides for any ham dish: buttered rice, glazed pineapple, fried eggs, hash brown potatoes, hominy, corn muffins, or fried bananas.

Bar-B-Q Ham & Beankraut

1   30-oz. can chili beans

1   16-oz. can sauerkraut

2   cups thinly sliced ham

1   cup COOKIES Original Bar-B-Q Sauce

½   cup chopped onion

1½ tbsp. chopped green sweet pepper

1½ tbsp. chopped red sweet pepper

1. Combine all ingredients in a large skillet. Heat to boiling; reduce heat. Simmer, covered, for 15 minutes or until onion is tender.
Makes: 6 to 8 servings

Ham Balls

2   eggs, beaten

2   cups crushed graham crackers

1   cup milk

2½ cups COOKIES Original Bar-B-Q Sauce

2   lbs. ground ham

1   lb. ground pork sausage

1. Mix eggs, graham crackers, milk, and ½ cup of the Bar-B-Q Sauce in a large bowl. Add ham and sausage; mix well. Form into 40 balls and place in a 13×9×2-inch baking pan. Cover with remaining 2 cups Bar-B-Q Sauce. Bake, uncovered, in a 350° oven for 1½ hours or until glazed and cooked through (160°).
Makes: 8 main-dish servings

Franks & Rice

3   cups cooked rice

6   frankfurters

1   10¾-oz. can reduced-fat and reduced-sodium
    condensed vegetable soup

¼   cup COOKIES Original Bar-B-Q Sauce

2   tbsp. water

1   tsp. Worcestershire sauce

¼   tsp. COOKIES Flavor Enhancer
    Dash COOKIES Wings-N-Things Hot Sauce

1. Place cooked rice in a greased 1½-quart casserole. Top with frankfurters. Mix soup, Bar-B-Q Sauce, water, Worcestershire sauce, Flavor Enhancer, and Wings-N-Things. Pour soup mixture over frankfurters and rice. Bake, uncovered, in a 375° oven for 25 to 30 minutes or until heated through.
Makes: 6 servings

Oven-Baked Wieners

10   wieners

1   small onion, diced

2   tbsp. butter, melted

1½   cups COOKIES Original Bar-B-Q Sauce

1. Split wieners lengthwise. Place in a shallow casserole with split sides up. Sprinkle with onion and drizzle with butter. Cover with Bar-B-Q Sauce. Bake, uncovered, in a 350° oven for 30 minutes.
Makes: 4 servings

Gyros Roast

1   1½-lb. boneless lamb leg roast
1   2½-lb. boneless beef round steak
2   cups dry white wine
¼   cup dried oregano
2   tsp. dried dill weed
½   tsp. ground thyme
2   tsp. garlic powder
2   tsp. COOKIES Flavor Enhancer
    Olive oil
⅓   cup COOKIES Original Bar-B-Q Sauce

1. Place lamb and beef round steak between waxed paper and pound with flat side of a meat mallet until each piece of meat measures about 12×14 inches. Place in a plastic bag set in a large bowl and pour wine over meat; seal bag and refrigerate overnight.

2. Combine herbs, garlic powder, and Flavor Enhancer, crushing with back of spoon. Remove lamb from wine and place on cutting board; brush top lightly with oil and sprinkle with half of the herb mixture. Cover with waxed paper and pound herbs into the surface of lamb with meat mallet. Remove waxed paper and lay round steak on top of lamb; brush top with Bar-B-Q Sauce. Sprinkle with a third of the herb mixture. Cover and pound herbs into surface of beef with meat mallet. Roll up meats as tightly as possible, starting at a short end; tie securely in several places with string. Brush outside of roast lightly with Bar-B-Q Sauce; rub with remaining herb mixture.

3. Insert meat thermometer so that tip is in center of meat. Arrange medium coals around a drip pan; place roast over drip pan. Grill, covered, about 1½ hours or until internal temperature registers 135° for medium rare. Remove meat from grill; cover with foil and let stand for 15 minutes before serving (the meat's temperature will rise 10°).
Makes: 12 to 16 servings

Lamb Shanks

¼   cup all-purpose flour
½   tsp. COOKIES Flavor Enhancer
4   lamb shanks
2   tbsp. shortening
2   cups COOKIES Original Bar-B-Q Sauce

1. Mix flour and Flavor Enhancer. Coat lamb shanks with flour mixture. Heat shortening in a large skillet. Brown shanks in hot shortening. Place shanks in a large, shallow baking dish. Cover with Bar-B-Q Sauce. Bake in a 350° oven for 1½ to 2 hours or until tender.
Makes: 4 servings

Lamb Burgers

1	egg, beaten
1	cup COOKIES Original Bar-B-Q Sauce
½	cup oatmeal
1	tbsp. milk
½	tsp. garlic salt
½	tsp. COOKIES Flavor Enhancer
2	lbs. ground lamb

1. In a large bowl, combine egg, Bar-B-Q Sauce, oatmeal, milk, garlic salt, and Flavor Enhancer; add lamb and mix well. Shape into six ½-inch-thick burgers. Grill directly over medium coals for 10 to 13 minutes (160°).
Makes: 6 servings

Lamb Kabobs

2	lbs. boneless leg of lamb
1	cup COOKIES Original Bar-B-Q Sauce
1	large onion, diced
1	small carrot, diced
2	tbsp. chopped fresh parsley
½	tsp. COOKIES Flavor Enhancer
12	cherry tomatoes
	Hot cooked rice

1. Cut lamb into 1-inch cubes; place in a large bowl. Mix Bar-B-Q Sauce, onion, carrot, parsley, and Flavor Enhancer; pour over the lamb. Stir to coat all pieces evenly. Cover and refrigerate for 2 hours, stirring every 30 minutes. Remove lamb from marinade and thread on 12 skewers. Place a tomato at the ends of each skewer. Grill directly over medium coals for 8 to 12 minutes or to desired doneness, turning occasionally to brown evenly. Baste with the marinade during the first 5 minutes of grilling. Serve with rice.
Makes: 6 servings

CHICKEN, TURKEY & FISH

Chapter 5

Bar-B-Q Beer Chicken

1   12-oz. can beer

½   cup butter

3   tbsp. COOKIES Flavor Enhancer

1   3-lb. broiler-fryer chicken, cut up

1   18-oz. bottle COOKIES Original Bar-B-Q Sauce

1. Heat beer, butter, and Flavor Enhancer in a saucepan until butter melts. Remove from heat; set aside. Arrange medium hot coals around a drip pan. Dip chicken pieces in beer mixture and place over the drip pan. Grill, covered, for 50 to 60 minutes or until tender (180°), basting occasionally with beer mixture during the first 30 minutes. During the last 10 minutes, baste chicken with Bar-B-Q Sauce.

Makes: 4 to 6 servings

No-Peek Bar-B-Qued Chicken

3   lbs. meaty chicken pieces

1   18-oz. bottle COOKIES Original Bar-B-Q Sauce

1   tsp. COOKIES Flavor Enhancer

1   can sauerkraut (optional)

1. Dip chicken in Bar-B-Q Sauce to coat all sides; place in a 13×9×2-inch baking pan. Sprinkle Flavor Enhancer on top of chicken and pour on the rest of the Bar-B-Q Sauce. Cover tightly with foil. Bake in a 350° oven about 1 hour (180°). If desired, sprinkle sauerkraut over the chicken 10 minutes before it is done.

Makes: 4 to 6 servings

COOKIES Bar-B-Qued Cornish Hens

1   18-oz. bottle **COOKIES Original Bar-B-Q Sauce**

1   16-oz. can whole cranberry sauce

2   tbsp. diced onion

1   tsp. yellow or Dijon-style mustard

2   1¼- to 1½-lb. Cornish game hens

1. Mix Bar-B-Q Sauce, cranberry sauce, onion, and mustard in a medium bowl. Cut hens in half lengthwise. Arrange medium coals around a drip pan. Brush hens with some of the sauce mixture; place, cut side down, over the drip pan. Grill, covered, for 40 to 50 minutes (180°), basting with sauce mixture occasionally during the first 30 minutes. If desired, heat any remaining sauce to boiling and pass with hens.

Makes: 4 servings

the **"SAUCEMAN"** says

To avoid tears when peeling onions, peel them under cold water or refrigerate before chopping.

Del Rio Hens

1   18-oz. bottle **COOKIES Taco Sauce & Dip**

1   12-oz. jar orange marmalade

4   1¼- to 1½-lb. Cornish game hens

1. In a small saucepan, bring Taco Sauce and orange marmalade to a boil. Place hens on a foil-lined baking pan and spoon sauce over all. Bake, uncovered, in a 375° oven for 1¼ to 1½ hours or until hens are tender (180°), spooning sauce over occasionally.

Makes: 4 servings

Chicken Sloppy Joes

1   3-lb. broiler-fryer chicken, cut up

1   tsp. COOKIES Flavor Enhancer

1   small green sweet pepper, diced

1   small onion, diced

2   14-oz. cans chicken broth

2   cups COOKIES Original Bar-B-Q Sauce

⅓   cup water

3   tbsp. cornstarch

     Hamburger buns, split and toasted,
       or toasted sliced bread

1. Sprinkle chicken with Flavor Enhancer and place in a 3½- to 4-quart slow cooker; add green pepper, onion, and chicken broth. Cook, covered, on high-heat setting for 4 to 6 hours or until chicken is very tender. Remove chicken; cool slightly.

2. When cool enough to handle, skin chicken and remove from bones; discard skin and bones. Shred chicken. Place chicken in a large skillet with Bar-B-Q Sauce. Heat just to boiling. Mix water and cornstarch and add to chicken mixture. Cook and stir until thickened and bubbly; cook and stir for 2 minutes more. Serve on buns or over bread.
Makes: 6 to 8 servings

Slow Cooked Chicken

2   tbsp. shortening

1   tsp. COOKIES Flavor Enhancer

1   3-lb. broiler-fryer chicken, cut up

2   cups COOKIES Original Bar-B-Q Sauce

½   cup water

1. Melt shortening in a skillet over medium heat. Sprinkle Flavor Enhancer on chicken and brown in hot shortening; drain chicken. Place in 3½- to 4-quart slow cooker. Mix Bar-B-Q Sauce and water; pour mixture over the chicken. Cook, covered, on low-heat setting for 6 to 7 hours. Chicken should be very tender.
Makes: 4 to 6 servings

Creole Chicken

10	slices bacon
⅓	cup all-purpose flour
½	tsp. COOKIES Flavor Enhancer
2	lbs. meaty chicken pieces
1	tbsp. olive oil
¾	cup chopped onion
1	cup chopped celery
1	small green sweet pepper, chopped
3	cups COOKIES Original Bar-B-Q Sauce
1	cup water
3	cups cooked rice

1. Fry bacon in a stew pot until crispy. Drain bacon on paper towels, reserving 2 tablespoons drippings in pot. Mix flour and Flavor Enhancer. Dredge chicken in flour mixture and fry in reserved drippings until golden brown. Remove from pot. Add olive oil and onion. Cook for 5 minutes; add celery and green pepper. Cook another 4 minutes; add Bar-B-Q Sauce and water. Bring to boiling; place chicken pieces in pot. Simmer, covered, for 40 minutes. Serve chicken pieces over rice with sauce from pan spooned over the chicken.
Makes: 4 to 6 servings

the "SAUCEMAN" says

Rice will be fluffier and whiter if you add 1 teaspoon of lemon juice to each quart of the water used for boiling.

Double Bar-B-Q Chicken

1	3-lb. broiler-fryer chicken, cut up
1	tsp. COOKIES Flavor Enhancer
1	18-oz. bottle COOKIES Original Bar-B-Q Sauce
1	bag barbecue-flavored potato chips, crushed

1. Sprinkle chicken with Flavor Enhancer. Roll chicken in half of the Bar-B-Q Sauce, then in crushed chips to coat. Place chicken in a single layer in a lightly greased shallow baking pan. Bake in a 375° oven for 45 to 55 minutes or until tender (180°). Serve with remaining half of Bar-B-Q Sauce.
Makes: 4 to 6 servings

Dinner for Four

1   cup COOKIES Taco Sauce & Dip

½   cup uncooked rice

¼   cup chopped salad olives
     (green and pimiento)

½   tsp. dried celery leaves, crushed

1   2½-lb. broiler-fryer chicken, cut up

1   pkg. onion soup mix

1. Mix Taco Sauce, rice, olives, and celery leaves. Pour into a well-greased 13×9×2-inch baking pan. Arrange chicken pieces on top of rice mixture, overlapping as little as possible. Sprinkle onion soup mix over the top of the chicken. Cover pan tightly with aluminum foil. Bake in a 350° oven for 2 hours or until chicken and rice are tender. No peeking!

Makes: 4 servings

Grilled Chicken

1   tbsp. COOKIES Flavor Enhancer

1   3-lb. broiler-fryer chicken, cut up

2   cups COOKIES Original Bar-B-Q Sauce

1. Sprinkle Flavor Enhancer over chicken. Grill chicken directly over medium coals for 35 to 45 minutes or until tender, basting frequently with Bar-B-Q Sauce. (Watch closely to avoid flare-ups.) Heat remaining sauce and pass with chicken.

Makes: 4 to 6 servings

Honey Bar-B-Qued Chicken

1½	cups COOKIES Original Bar-B-Q Sauce
½	cup mayonnaise
½	cup honey
3	tbsp. pineapple juice
2	tbsp. soy sauce
1	tbsp. lemon juice
½	tsp. paprika
½	tsp. COOKIES Flavor Enhancer
1	3-lb. broiler-fryer chicken, cut up

1. Mix all ingredients except chicken. Place chicken in a shallow baking pan. Cover with Bar-B-Q Sauce mixture. Bake, uncovered, in a 350° oven for 30 minutes. Turn pieces over. Return to oven and bake for 30 to 40 minutes more or until tender.
Makes: 4 to 6 servings

Japanese Spiced Chicken

3	2-lb. broiler-fryer chickens, split in half
1	18-oz. bottle COOKIES Original Bar-B-Q Sauce
1	cup soy sauce
¼	cup dry sherry
2	tbsp. lemon juice
½	tsp. ground ginger
2	cloves garlic, crushed

1. Place chicken in a large flat dish or pan. Combine remaining ingredients and pour over chicken. Marinate, covered, in refrigerator for 2 hours, turning chicken pieces occasionally. Drain chicken, reserving marinade. Arrange medium-hot coals around a drip pan; place chicken pieces, bone side down, over drip pan. Grill, covered, for 1 to 1¼ hours or until tender, brushing with reserved marinade several times during the first 30 minutes of grilling (discard any remaining marinade).
Makes: 6 servings

the "SAUCEMAN" says

Chop garlic in a small amount of salt to prevent pieces from sticking to the knife or the chopping board; then pulverize garlic with the tip of the knife to crush.

Grilled Chicken in Aluminum Foil

2 cups COOKIES Original Bar-B-Q Sauce

½ cup margarine, melted

¼ cup ketchup

2 tbsp. Worcestershire sauce

3 tbsp. lemon juice

¼ cup Heinz 57 Sauce

½ tsp. COOKIES Flavor Enhancer

½ tsp. dry mustard

1 tbsp. brown sugar

1 3-lb. broiler-fryer chicken, cut up

1. Combine all ingredients except chicken in a medium saucepan. Bring to a boil. Arrange medium-hot coals around a drip pan. Grill chicken directly over the coals for 5 minutes per side just until brown. Remove from grill and dip in sauce mixture. Place each chicken piece on a sheet of heavy duty foil; add a little more of the sauce mixture and wrap up foil to enclose. Place packets on the grill drip pan; grill, covered, for 40 minutes or until chicken is tender (open packets carefully). Reheat remaining sauce mixture to boiling and pass with chicken.

Makes: 4 to 6 servings

Pop Goes the Chicken

1 tbsp. shortening

1 3-lb. broiler-fryer chicken, cut up

1 12-oz. can Pepsi

1½ cups COOKIES Original Bar-B-Q Sauce

1. Place shortening in an electric skillet; turn to 350°. (Or use a large skillet and heat over medium heat.) Carefully place chicken in skillet and cook about 10 minutes, turning to brown evenly; drain fat. Carefully add Pepsi and Bar-B-Q Sauce. Heat to boiling; reduce heat. Simmer, covered, for 35 to 40 minutes or until tender (180°), spooning sauce over chicken occasionally.

Makes: 4 to 6 servings

the "SAUCEMAN" says

When you want a crisp, brown crust on chicken, rub mayonnaise over it before grilling or baking.

Spicy Cornflake Chicken

1   3-lb. broiler-fryer chicken, cut up
1   bottle COOKIES Western Style Bar-B-Q Sauce
1½   cups crushed cornflakes

1. Dip chicken in Bar-B-Q Sauce and roll in crushed cornflakes to coat. Place in a 15×10×1-inch baking pan and bake in a 375° oven for 45 to 55 minutes or until tender.
Makes: 4 to 6 servings

Sweet & Sour Chicken

¼   cup all-purpose flour
½   tsp. COOKIES Flavor Enhancer
1   3-lb. broiler-fryer chicken, cut up
2   tbsp. cooking oil
1   8-oz. can crushed pineapple
1   18-oz. bottle COOKIES Original Bar-B-Q Sauce
½   tsp. ground ginger

1. Combine flour and Flavor Enhancer. Coat chicken with flour mixture. Brown chicken in hot oil in a large skillet over medium heat. Combine pineapple, Bar-B-Q Sauce, and ginger. Add sauce mixture to chicken. Heat to boiling; reduce heat. Simmer, covered, for 35 to 45 minutes or until chicken is tender.
Makes: 4 to 6 servings

Mustard-Baked Chicken

2½ lbs. meaty chicken pieces

½ cup maple honey-flavored syrup

¼ cup yellow mustard

2 tbsp. lemon juice

¾ tsp. COOKIES Flavor Enhancer

¼ cup margarine, melted

1. Place chicken pieces in shallow pan. Combine syrup, mustard, lemon juice, and Flavor Enhancer. Spoon over chicken, turning to coat both sides. Cover and refrigerate for at least 2 hours or overnight; drain chicken, reserving marinade. Place chicken, skin side up, in shallow baking dish. Drizzle melted margarine over chicken. Bake, uncovered, in a 350° oven for 30 minutes. Increase oven temperature to 400° and continue baking 20 to 30 minutes longer or until chicken is tender, basting frequently with drippings. Place chicken on platter and keep warm. Combine drippings and reserved marinade in saucepan. Heat until bubbly and slightly thickened. Serve with chicken.

Makes: 6 servings

Tipsy Chicken

1 3-lb. whole chicken

COOKIES Flavor Enhancer

1 12-oz. can beer

Nonstick cooking spray

1. Sprinkle chicken cavity with Flavor Enhancer. Pour half of the beer out of the can and discard. Hold the chicken upright with the opening of the body cavity at the bottom and lower it onto the beer can so the can fits into the cavity. Pull the chicken legs forward so the bird rests on its legs and the can. Twist wing tips behind back. Spray chicken with cooking spray and sprinkle generously with additional Flavor Enhancer.

2. Arrange medium-hot coals around a drip pan. Stand chicken upright on grill rack over drip pan. Grill, covered, for 1 to 1¼ hours or until chicken is no longer pink (180° in thigh muscle). If necessary, tent chicken with foil to prevent overbrowning. Remove chicken from grill, holding by the can. Cover chicken with foil; let stand for 10 minutes. Use a hot pad to grasp can and heavy tongs to carefully remove the chicken.

Makes: 4 to 6 servings

Baked Salsa Chicken

4   skinless, boneless chicken breast halves

1   jar COOKIES Premium Salsa, mild or medium

1   cup fat-free shredded cheddar cheese

1   to 2 tbsp. nonfat sour cream

    Corn tortillas (optional)

1. Place chicken in an 8×8×2-inch baking pan. Cover with Salsa. Bake in a 375° oven for 30 to 45 minutes. Top with cheese; broil 3 to 4 inches from the heat for 3 to 5 minutes to brown cheese. Garnish with sour cream and more Salsa. If desired, wrap chicken mixture in corn tortillas to serve.

Makes: 4 servings

Boneless Chicken Breasts

3   skinless, boneless chicken breasts

½   cup COOKIES Original Bar-B-Q Sauce

½   cup creamy Italian salad dressing

¼   cup orange juice

    Wood chips

1. Place chicken in a plastic bag set in a large bowl. Combine Bar-B-Q Sauce, salad dressing, and orange juice; pour over chicken. Seal bag and refrigerate overnight. Soak wood chips in enough water to cover for at least 1 hour; drain. Arrange medium-hot coals around a drip pan; sprinkle drained wood chips over coals. Drain chicken, discarding marinade. Place chicken on grill over drip pan. Grill, covered, for 20 to 30 minutes or until tender.

Makes: 3 servings

the "SAUCEMAN" says

Fried or baked chicken is especially delicious when it has been marinated in the refrigerator overnight in buttermilk, sour milk, or sour cream.

Chicken Mexicali-Style

2   lbs. skinless, boneless chicken breast
    halves (6 to 8)
1   cup COOKIES Taco Sauce & Dip
1   16-oz. can stewed tomatoes
½   cup chopped onion
½   tsp. COOKIES Flavor Enhancer
¼   tsp. garlic powder
¼   tsp. dried oregano
2   cups shredded cheddar cheese

1. Place chicken in an ungreased 9×9×2-inch baking pan. Mix Taco Sauce, tomatoes, onion, Flavor Enhancer, garlic powder, and oregano; pour over chicken. Bake, uncovered, in a 350° oven for 1¼ hours or until tender. Remove from oven and add cheese. Bake for 5 to 10 minutes more or until golden brown.
Makes: 6 to 8 servings

Pineapple Chicken

6   skinless, boneless chicken breast halves
2   cups pineapple juice
1   tbsp. lemon juice
½   tsp. COOKIES Flavor Enhancer
1   cup drained, canned pineapple tidbits
½   cup light-colored corn syrup
1   cup COOKIES Original Bar-B-Q Sauce

1. Place chicken breasts in a plastic bag set in a large bowl; add pineapple and lemon juices. Refrigerate for 6 hours; drain. Place breasts in lightly greased 13×9×2-inch baking pan; sprinkle with Flavor Enhancer. Add pineapple tidbits. Drizzle with corn syrup. Gently pour Bar-B-Q Sauce over chicken. Bake, uncovered, in a 375° oven for 30 minutes. Baste with juices. Bake for 15 to 25 minutes more or until chicken is tender.
Makes: 6 servings

the "SAUCEMAN" says

For a great complement to baked chicken, try pairing it with candied sweet potatoes and cauliflower.

Far West Chicken

1   red onion, chopped

½   cup unsweetened pineapple juice

¼   cup fresh cilantro, chopped

1   jalapeño pepper, minced

1   tsp. fresh lime juice

1   tsp. red wine vinegar

2   tsp. paprika

2   tsp. dried oregano

2   tsp. dried thyme

½   tsp. COOKIES Flavor Enhancer

½   tsp. cayenne pepper

1½ lbs. skinless, boneless chicken breast halves

¾   lb. fresh pineapple slices
        (about 1 small pineapple)

2   tsp. canola oil

1. For salsa, in medium bowl, combine onion, pineapple juice, cilantro, jalapeño pepper, lime juice, and vinegar. Set aside at room temperature. In a small bowl, combine the paprika, oregano, thyme, Flavor Enhancer, and cayenne. Use your fingers to coat the chicken and the pineapple slices lightly with the oil, then sprinkle the chicken with the seasoning blend. Grill the chicken for 12 to 15 minutes or until tender, turning once. Grill the pineapple for 2 to 3 minutes or until lightly browned, turning once. Coarsely dice the pineapple slices and add to the salsa. Arrange the chicken on a platter or individual plates. Spoon some of the salsa on top and the remainder on the side.
Makes: 6 servings

Rice Krispies Chicken

1   family pack chicken

¼   cup margarine, melted

2   cups crushed Rice Krispies

1   tsp. COOKIES Flavor Enhancer

1½ to 2 cups COOKIES Original Bar-B-Q Sauce

1. Dip chicken pieces in margarine, then in crushed Rice Krispies. Lay chicken in a 15×10×1-inch baking pan; sprinkle with Flavor Enhancer. Bake, uncovered, in a 350° oven for 45 to 60 minutes or until tender. Meanwhile, heat Bar-B-Q Sauce; pass with chicken.
Makes: 4 to 6 servings

Cheesy Chicken Roll-Ups

6   skinless, boneless chicken breast halves
10   oz. shredded Swiss cheese (2½ cups)
2   eggs, beaten
3   tbsp. seasoned fine dry bread crumbs
3   tbsp. dried parsley flakes
½   tsp. COOKIES Flavor Enhancer
2   tbsp. cooking oil
2   cups COOKIES Original Bar-B-Q Sauce

1. Place chicken pieces between sheets of plastic wrap; pound with the flat side of a meat mallet until ¼ inch thick. Combine cheese, eggs, bread crumbs, parsley, and Flavor Enhancer. Place one-sixth of the mixture on each chicken breast. Roll up and secure with toothpicks.

2. In a large skillet, heat oil. Brown chicken, turning to brown all sides. Pour Bar-B-Q Sauce over chicken. Heat to boiling; reduce heat. Simmer, covered, for 35 to 45 minutes or until tender.
Makes: 6 servings

Chicken Cordon Blue

6   skinless, boneless chicken breast halves
1   8-oz. pkg. mozzarella cheese,
        cut into 6 large cubes
1   small ham slice, cut into 6 large cubes
½   cup COOKIES Original Bar-B-Q Sauce
1   tbsp. Worcestershire sauce
1   tbsp. Dijon-style mustard
½   tsp. garlic powder
    Lemon Rice

1. Place chicken between plastic wrap; pound lightly with the flat side of a meat mallet until about ⅛ inch thick. Place 1 cube of mozzarella cheese and 1 cube of ham on each chicken piece. Fold in bottom and sides and roll up; secure with toothpicks. Place in shallow baking dish. Mix Bar-B-Q Sauce, Worcestershire sauce, mustard, and garlic powder. Pour over chicken rolls; cover and refrigerate for 2 to 3 hours. Drain off marinade; remove chicken. Wash baking dish and return chicken to dish. Bake, uncovered, in 400° oven for 15 to 18 minutes or until tender. Serve with Lemon Rice.
Makes: 6 servings

Lemon Rice: Cook 1 cup long grain rice according to package directions. Add 1 tablespoon butter. Drizzle 1 tablespoon lemon juice over each serving.

COOKIES Wings-N-Things Fettuccine

2 lbs. fettuccine

4 skinless, boneless chicken breast halves

¼ cup diced red sweet peppers

¼ cup diced green sweet peppers

2 tbsp. chopped green onions

2 tbsp. chopped fresh parsley

½ cup butter, melted

½ cup COOKIES Wings-N-Things Hot Sauce

1. Prepare pasta according to package directions; drain. Meanwhile, grill chicken directly over medium coals for 12 to 15 minutes or until tender, turning once. Chop chicken. Combine chicken, peppers, onions, parsley, and cooked fettuccine; toss to mix. Drizzle with butter and toss to coat. Drizzle Wings-N-Things over top and serve.

Makes: 6 servings

the "SAUCEMAN" says

Fresh parsley will keep a long time in the refrigerator if, after washing it, you place it in a covered jar while still slightly damp.

Macho Pollo

6 skinless, boneless chicken breast halves

¼ tsp. COOKIES Flavor Enhancer

½ cup coarsely chopped Spanish green olives

2 tbsp. chopped green chiles

2½ cups grated cheddar cheese

2 eggs, slightly beaten

1 cup crushed tortilla chips

1 18-oz. bottle COOKIES Taco Sauce & Dip

1. Place each breast half between 2 sheets of plastic wrap and pound with the flat side of a meat mallet until very thin. Sprinkle each breast with Flavor Enhancer. Mix olives, chiles, and 2 cups of the cheese. Spread one-sixth of this mixture on each breast half. Roll up chicken, jelly roll-style. Dip each chicken roll in beaten eggs, then in crushed tortilla chips. Place rolls in a 2-quart rectangular baking dish and cover with Taco Sauce. Sprinkle the remaining ½ cup cheese over the pan. Bake in 350° oven for 45 to 60 minutes or until tender.

Makes: 6 servings

Chicken Quesadillas

1   lb. skinless, boneless chicken breast
    halves, cubed
1   11-oz. can condensed cheddar cheese soup
½   cup COOKIES Premium Salsa
10 7- or 8-inch flour tortillas

1. Cook chicken in skillet in hot oil until tender. Add soup and Salsa; heat through. Spread ⅓ cup chicken mixture on half of each tortilla to within ½ inch of edge. Moisten edge with water. Fold over and seal. Place prepared tortillas on 2 baking sheets. Bake in 425° oven for 5 minutes or until hot.
Makes: 5 servings

Easy Chicken Chow Mein

1   10-oz. pkg. frozen Chinese vegetables
2   3-oz. pkgs. Asian-style noodles
¼   tsp. COOKIES Flavor Enhancer
6   skinless, boneless chicken breast halves
2   tbsp. cooking oil
¼   cup COOKIES Original Bar-B-Q Sauce
1   tsp. soy sauce

1. Cook frozen vegetables in boiling water for 5 minutes. Cook Asian-style noodles with Flavor Enhancer in boiling water for 3 minutes (discard seasoning packets). Cut chicken breasts into bite-size pieces. In wok or large skillet, heat oil over high heat and stir-fry chicken about 4 minutes or until tender. Add cooked vegetables, noodles, Bar-B-Q Sauce, and soy sauce to chicken. Stir until well mixed and thoroughly heated.
Makes: 4 to 6 servings

Chicken Cacciatore

2   lbs. skinless, boneless chicken breast halves

3   tbsp. butter

1   onion, diced

2   cups COOKIES Original Bar-B-Q Sauce

1   cup dry sherry

⅔   cup water

¼   cup lemon juice

2   tbsp. Worcestershire sauce

1   8-oz. pkg. egg noodles, cooked and drained

1. Cut chicken into bite-size pieces. Heat butter in a large skillet over medium heat. Brown chicken and onion. Add remaining ingredients except noodles. Heat to boiling; reduce heat. Simmer, uncovered, until chicken is tender and sauce is slightly thickened. Serve over noodles.
Makes: 4 servings

Croissant Taco Chicken Casserole

2   8-oz. tubes refrigerated crescent rolls

3   cups shredded cooked chicken breasts

1   10-oz. can enchilada sauce

1   cup COOKIES Taco Sauce & Dip

1   8-oz. carton sour cream

1   1¼-oz. pkg. taco seasoning

2   cups shredded cheddar cheese

Shredded lettuce

Crushed Doritos

1. Press crescent rolls in bottom of a 13×9×2-inch baking pan, pressing seams to seal. Combine chicken, enchilada sauce, Taco Sauce, sour cream, and taco seasoning; spread over crust. Top with cheddar cheese. Bake in 350° oven for 30 minutes or until heated through and crust is browned on bottom. Serve warm, topped with lettuce and crushed Doritos.
Makes: 6 servings

the "SAUCEMAN" says

To keep sour cream fresh longer, store container upside down in the refrigerator so that air cannot escape.

Sour Cream Chicken Enchiladas

2	cups chopped cooked chicken
1	16-oz. carton sour cream
1	10¾-oz. can condensed cream of chicken soup
¾	cup finely chopped onion
¾	cup finely chopped green sweet pepper
24	6- to 8-inch corn or flour tortillas
1	lb. shredded Monterey Jack cheese
1	lb. shredded Colby cheese
1	cup COOKIES Taco Sauce & Dip
	Chopped green sweet pepper (optional)
	Chopped pitted ripe olives (optional)

1. Mix chicken, sour cream, soup, onion, and finely chopped green pepper. Spread about one-third of the chicken mixture on the bottom of a lightly greased 13×9×2-inch baking pan. Wrap tortillas in foil and heat in a 300° oven for 10 to 15 minutes to warm slightly. Place a generous tablespoon of chicken mixture on each tortilla, along with a tablespoon of each cheese. Roll up and place, seam side down, in the baking pan. Top with Taco Sauce. Sprinkle with remaining cheeses. If desired, sprinkle with chopped pepper and black olives. Bake, uncovered, at 300° for 35 to 45 minutes or until heated through.
Makes: 4 to 6 servings

Spicy Chicken Noodle Dinner

½	of a 12-oz. pkg. egg noodles
¾	cup chopped green sweet pepper
¼	cup chopped onion
1	tsp. curry powder
1	tbsp. margarine
¼	cup all-purpose flour
3	cups skim milk
2	cups chopped cooked chicken
1	3-oz. can sliced mushrooms, drained
1	tsp. dried parsley flakes
1	tsp. COOKIES Flavor Enhancer
	Dash COOKIES Wings-N-Things Hot Sauce

1. Prepare noodles according to package directions; drain and rinse. Sauté green pepper, onion, and curry powder in margarine until tender. Add flour; stir in milk. Cook, stirring constantly, until slightly thickened and bubbly. Add chicken, mushrooms, parsley, Flavor Enhancer, and Wings-N-Things. Cook and stir for 5 minutes more. Serve over noodles.
Makes: 4 servings

the "SAUCEMAN" says

Each time there is just a small amount of vegetable left over from a meal, add it to a designated "For Soup" container in the freezer. Later, add to a pot of soup without wasting vegetables.

Cheddar Turkey Loaf

2   eggs, beaten
⅔   cup COOKIES Original Bar-B-Q Sauce
1   11-oz. can condensed cheddar cheese soup
6   slices thin sandwich bread,
          torn into small pieces
¾   cup diced onion
3   strips turkey bacon, cooked and crumbled
2   jalapeño peppers, seeded and finely chopped
1   tsp. salt
½   tsp. black pepper
½   tsp. garlic powder
1½   lbs. uncooked ground turkey

1. Mix eggs, ⅓ cup of the Bar-B-Q Sauce, soup, bread, onion, bacon, jalapeño peppers, salt, pepper, and garlic powder. Add turkey and mix well. Place in an 8×8×2-inch baking dish. Spread remaining ⅓ cup Bar-B-Q Sauce over the top of the meat and bake in a 350° oven for 1½ hours (180°). Let stand 10 minutes before serving.
Makes: 6 servings

Turkey Wraps

12   10-inch flour tortillas
2   lbs. shredded cooked turkey
¼   cup COOKIES Premium Salsa
1   16-oz. carton sour cream
       COOKIES Premium Salsa (optional)
       Shredded cheddar cheese (optional)

1. Wrap tortillas in foil and heat in a 300° oven for 10 to 15 minutes or until warm. In a saucepan, heat turkey and Salsa. Spread some sour cream and turkey mixture on each tortilla. If desired, top with additional Salsa and some cheese. Roll up and serve. This is a great way to use leftovers.
Makes: 12 servings

Creamy Salsa Turkey

2 tbsp. margarine
¼ tsp. COOKIES Flavor Enhancer
1 lb. turkey breast slices
½ cup COOKIES Premium Salsa
2 tsp. soy sauce
1 tsp. lime juice
1 clove garlic, chopped
½ cup sour cream
2 green onions, sliced

1. Melt margarine in a skillet. Sprinkle Flavor Enhancer on both sides of turkey and cook in margarine for 3 to 5 minutes per side or until tender. Remove turkey and keep warm. In same skillet, combine Salsa, soy sauce, lime juice, and garlic. Heat to boiling, stirring constantly. Remove from heat and stir in sour cream. Pour over turkey and top with green onions.
Makes: 4 to 6 servings

Turkey Kabobs

6 cups vegetables (such as green sweet pepper squares, cauliflower or broccoli florets, small mushrooms, cherry tomatoes, quartered potatoes, onion wedges, or 1-inch slices of zucchini)
2 lbs. turkey tenderloins, cut into 1-inch cubes
1 cup COOKIES Original Bar-B-Q Sauce
1 cup Italian salad dressing
1 tbsp. white or red wine vinegar
1 tbsp. lemon juice
¾ tsp. onion salt
½ tsp. garlic powder
½ tsp. dried marjoram
⅛ tsp. black pepper
   Fresh or canned pineapple chunks (optional)

1. Blanch green peppers, cauliflower, broccoli, potatoes, and onions by adding to a large amount of boiling water; boil for 1 minute and drain. Use other vegetables unblanched. Place vegetables in a large plastic bag; set aside. Place turkey in another plastic bag; set aside. Combine Bar-B-Q Sauce, Italian dressing, wine vinegar, lemon juice, onion salt, garlic powder, marjoram, and pepper. Pour half the sauce mixture into each bag; seal and refrigerate overnight.

2. Drain. Alternately thread turkey, vegetables, and, if desired, pineapple on skewers. Grill directly over medium coals for 12 to 15 minutes or until turkey and vegetables are tender.
Makes: 8 to 10 servings

Hot Turkey Salad Buns

2   cups cubed cooked turkey

1   cup shredded cheddar cheese

½   cup COOKIES Original Bar-B-Q Sauce

¼   cup finely chopped celery

¼   cup roasted almonds, chopped

1   finely chopped sweet pickle

¼   tsp. COOKIES Flavor Enhancer

4   large buns

1. Mix all ingredients except buns. Spoon about ½ cup turkey mixture onto each bun. Wrap in heavy duty foil. Arrange medium-hot coals around edges of grill; place sandwiches in center of grill, not over coals. Grill, covered, for 20 to 30 minutes or until heated through. (Or bake at 350° for 20 to 30 minutes.)

Makes: 4 servings

Legal Sloppy Joes

1½   lbs. uncooked ground turkey

¾   cup COOKIES Original Bar-B-Q Sauce

½   tsp. COOKIES Flavor Enhancer

6   sandwich buns

1. Brown turkey in skillet; drain fat. Add Bar-B-Q Sauce and Flavor Enhancer. Heat to boiling; reduce heat. Simmer for 5 to 10 minutes. Use ½ cup of meat for each sandwich.

Makes: 6 servings

Grilled Turkey Tenderloins

4   to 6 turkey tenderloins
1   cup COOKIES Original Bar-B-Q Sauce
½   cup dry sherry
¼   cup honey
¼   cup cooking oil
¼   cup lemon juice concentrate
½   tbsp. finely chopped onion
½   tsp. COOKIES Flavor Enhancer
¼   tsp. grated fresh ginger

1. Place turkey in a plastic bag set in a large bowl. Mix remaining ingredients and pour over turkey. Seal bag and refrigerate for 24 hours. Drain, discarding marinade. Grill directly over medium coals about 20 minutes or until tender, turning once.
Makes: 4 to 6 servings

Flavor-Enhanced Turkey

3   tbsp. COOKIES Flavor Enhancer
3   tbsp. garlic powder
    Dry white wine
1   12- to 14-lb. turkey

1. Mix Flavor Enhancer and garlic powder. Add enough white wine to make a paste. Remove neck and giblets from turkey. Rub the Flavor Enhancer mixture over the outside and inside of the turkey. Place in a large food grade plastic bag. Refrigerate overnight. Drain.

1. Pull neck skin to back and fasten with a skewer. If a band of skin crosses tail, tuck drumsticks under band. If there is no band, tie drumsticks to tail. Twist wing tips under the back. Arrange medium-hot coals around a drip pan; place turkey, breast side up, over the drip pan. Grill, covered, for 3 to 3¾ hours until thermometer inserted in inside thigh muscle registers 180°, adding coals as needed to maintain temperature. Remove from grill; cover with foil and let stand for 15 to 20 minutes before carving.
Makes: 12 to 14 servings

Note: If desired, place turkey on a rack in a roasting pan before placing it on the grill to make it easier to remove from grill. Using 2 wooden spoons works great for removing the hot turkey from the pan.

COOKIES Cajun-Style Turkey

2 large onions, chopped
2 large green sweet peppers, chopped
3 or 4 cloves garlic, minced
3 tbsp. COOKIES Wings-N-Things Hot Sauce
2 tbsp. hot mustard
2 tsp. vinegar
1 12- to 14-lb. turkey
1 small green sweet pepper,
       cut into 1-inch squares
1 18-oz. bottle COOKIES Taco Sauce & Dip

1. Mix onions, chopped green peppers, garlic, Wings-N-Things, mustard, and vinegar; cover and refrigerate overnight. Cut 4 to 5 slits about size of index finger into turkey breast. Each slit should reach the bone. Stuff the onion mixture into the slits. Cover slits with pieces of green pepper placed under the skin to keep the marinade in while cooking. Inject the breast with Taco Sauce.

2. Pull neck skin to back and fasten with a skewer. If a band of skin crosses tail, tuck drumsticks under band. If there is no band, tie drumsticks to tail. Twist wing tips under the back. Arrange medium-hot coals around a drip pan; place turkey, breast side up, over the drip pan. Grill, covered, for 3 to 3¾ hours until thermometer inserted in inside thigh muscle registers 180°, adding coals as needed to maintain temperature. Remove from grill; cover with foil and let stand 15 to 20 minutes before carving.
Makes: 12 to 14 servings

Slow Cooked Turkey

   Nonstick cooking spray
4 turkey breast tenderloins
½ tsp. COOKIES Flavor Enhancer
2 cups COOKIES Original Bar-B-Q Sauce
3 cups cooked rice

1. Spray a 2½- to 3½-quart slow cooker with cooking spray. Place turkey breasts on the bottom of the pot. Sprinkle on Flavor Enhancer. Pour on Bar-B-Q Sauce. Cook, covered, on low-heat setting for 4 hours. Serve on top of rice. Spoon sauce from cooker over the turkey and rice for extra flavor.
Makes: 4 servings

Bar-B-Qued Turkey

1	10- to 15-lb. turkey
1½	quarts COOKIES Original Bar-B-Q Sauce
¼	cup minced dried onion
2	tsp. liquid smoke
1	cup turkey broth

1. Roast turkey in a covered roasting pan in a 325° oven until meat falls easily from the bone (3 to 4 hours). Pour the cooking juices into a container and refrigerate. Discard solid fat from top of cooled juices. Discard turkey skin. Pull turkey from bone, keeping pieces about 2 to 3 inches long. Mix Bar-B-Q Sauce, dried onion, liquid smoke, and broth. Layer turkey in roaster. Cover each layer with the Bar-B-Q Sauce mixture. Repeat until all meat is used. Push turkey down and cover with the cooled cooking juices. Cover and heat through in a 250° oven. Serve hot or cold.

Makes: 12 to 15 servings

"SAUCEMAN" says

When preparing a turkey for a large group, assume each adult will eat ¼ to ½ pound of turkey. Children will eat ⅓ to ½ of that amount.

Bar-B-Qued Turkey Drumsticks

2	tbsp. cooking oil
4	1- to 1½-lb. turkey drumsticks
1	tsp. COOKIES Flavor Enhancer
4	cups COOKIES Original Bar-B-Q Sauce
1	cup water
¼	cup butter, melted

1. Heat oil in skillet and add drumsticks. Season with Flavor Enhancer and brown. Pour 2 cups of the Bar-B-Q Sauce and the water over drumsticks. Heat to boiling; reduce heat. Simmer, covered, almost 3 hours. Watch to see if water cooks away. If it does, add more. Heat oven to 425°. Put melted butter in a 13×9×2-inch baking pan; add drumsticks, turning to coat in butter. Bake, uncovered, for 15 minutes. Reduce heat to 350°. Pour remaining 2 cups Bar-B-Q Sauce over drumsticks and bake for 40 minutes more.

Makes: 4 drumsticks

Bar-B-Qued Catfish Fillets With Pecan Sauce

4   catfish, cod, or orange roughy fillets,
    ½ inch thick
    Juice of 1 lime
1   green sweet pepper
2   tbsp. butter
⅓   cup ground pecans
¾   cup COOKIES Original Bar-B-Q Sauce
2   ripe nectarines

1. Sprinkle both sides of fillets with lime juice and let stand for 5 minutes at room temperature. Clean and slice pepper into at least 8 thin rings. Place pepper rings in glass pie plate and dot with butter. Microwave on 100% power (high) for 1½ minutes. Remove and set aside. Dip fillets in ground pecans and place fish on another microwave-safe dish with thickest portion of fillets to outside. Pour on Bar-B-Q Sauce; cover with waxed paper. Microwave on 100% power (high) for 3½ minutes. Rotate dish and remove waxed paper. Slice nectarines in ¼-inch wedges. Arrange pepper rings and nectarine wedges around fish. Cover with waxed paper and microwave for 3 to 4 minutes more or until fish is opaque and flakes easily. Let stand, covered, for 3 minutes before serving.
Makes: 4 servings

Bar-B-Qued Fish Sandwiches

2   6-oz. cans tuna or crabmeat, well drained
1   cup COOKIES Original Bar-B-Q Sauce
    Dash COOKIES Flavor Enhancer
    Hamburger buns, split and toasted

1. Mix tuna, Bar-B-Q Sauce, and Flavor Enhancer. Stir gently over low heat until warm. Serve on hamburger buns.
Makes: 4 servings

Linguine with Clam Sauce

1   1-lb. package linguine
½   cup butter
¼   cup cooking oil
2   cloves garlic, minced
2   6½-oz. cans minced clams, drained
¼   cup fresh parsley, finely chopped
¼   tsp. dried basil
¼   tsp. COOKIES Flavor Enhancer
    Parmesan cheese

1. Prepare linguine according to package directions; drain and rinse. In a saucepan, heat butter and oil. Cook garlic and clams. Stir in parsley, basil, and Flavor Enhancer. Simmer for 5 minutes. Add hot linguine to clam mixture. Toss lightly. Serve on a warm platter. Sprinkle with Parmesan cheese.
Makes: 4 servings

"SAUCEMAN" says

Add a lump of butter or a few teaspoons of cooking oil to water to prevent rice, noodles, or spaghetti from boiling over and sticking together.

Cod Croquettes

1   lb. cooked cod fillets
2   cups mashed potatoes
    COOKIES Flavor Enhancer
    Dash grated nutmeg
1   egg
    Dry bread crumbs
    Oil for deep-fat frying
    Lettuce leaves
1   lemon, sliced or cut into wedges
    Tomato sauce

1. Finely grind cod and mix with potatoes. Season to taste with Flavor Enhancer and nutmeg. Shape cod mixture into small round or oval shapes. Lightly beat egg in a bowl. Dip croquettes in egg, then bread crumbs. Heat oil in deep-fryer to 360°. Add croquettes, 2 or 3 at a time, and fry for about 5 minutes or until golden brown. Remove and drain on paper towels. Pile croquettes on a bed of lettuce, with pieces of lemon between. Serve with tomato sauce.
Makes: 4 servings

Fish & Sauce

Butter-flavored Crisco
18   crappie or bluegill fillets
1½   cups COOKIES Original Bar-B-Q Sauce
½   tsp. COOKIES Flavor Enhancer
1   green sweet pepper, chopped
1   medium onion, chopped
3   slices Velveeta cheese, ⅛ inch thick

1. Grease a 13×9×2-inch baking dish with Crisco. Layer 6 fillets in bottom. Brush on Bar-B-Q Sauce; sprinkle with Flavor Enhancer. Sprinkle with one-third of the green pepper and onion. Repeat layers twice. Bake in a 350° oven for 20 minutes or until fish flakes easily when tested. Add cheese and bake for 3 to 5 minutes or until melted.
Makes: 6 servings

Combo Kabob

2   skinless, boneless chicken breast halves
6   large shrimp
2   8-oz. lobster tails, removed from shell
     and cut into pieces
2   6-oz. beef top sirloin steaks,
     cut into 6 pieces
2   onions, cut into wedges
1   fresh pineapple, cored and cut into chunks
8   oz. mushrooms
2   cups COOKIES Original Bar-B-Q Sauce

1. Cut chicken breasts into 6 pieces. On skewers, alternately thread shrimp, chicken, lobster, and steak pieces with the onions, pineapple, and mushrooms. Grill directly over medium coals for 15 to 20 minutes or until shrimp and lobster are opaque, chicken is tender, and beef is of desired doneness. Baste with Bar-B-Q Sauce while grilling.
Makes: 6 servings

Fresh Salmon Fillets

1⅓	cups COOKIES Original Bar-B-Q Sauce
⅔	cup diced onions
2	tbsp. butter, melted
2	tbsp. lemon juice
2	6-oz. salmon fillets, 1 inch thick

1. Mix Bar-B-Q Sauce, onions, butter, and lemon juice. Brush Bar-B-Q Sauce mixture over salmon fillets. Grill salmon directly over medium coals for 8 to 12 minutes or until fish flakes easily when tested. Brush with sauce occasionally. Heat remaining sauce to boiling and pass with fish.
Makes: 2 servings

the "SAUCEMAN" says

Citrus fruit yields nearly twice the amount of juice if it is dropped into hot water for a few minutes or rolled between your hands before squeezing.

Kahuna Tuna

1	medium onion, coarsely chopped
1	green sweet pepper, coarsely chopped
4	jalapeño peppers, seeded and chopped
3	cloves garlic, minced
1	tbsp. ground cumin
1	tbsp. dried basil
1	tbsp. black pepper
½	tsp. ground cinnamon
1	bay leaf
	Juice of 2 limes
3	lbs. fresh yellowfin tuna steaks, 1 inch thick
1	18-oz. bottle COOKIES Original Bar-B-Q Sauce

1. In a large skillet, cook onion, green pepper, jalapeño peppers, garlic, cumin, basil, pepper, cinnamon, and bay leaf over medium-high heat until charred. Add lime juice; let cool completely. Pour over tuna in a shallow dish; cover and refrigerate for 3 hours. Drain fish and transfer marinade to a medium saucepan. Add Bar-B-Q Sauce and bring to a boil.

2. Grill tuna directly over medium coals for 8 to 12 minutes or until fish flakes easily when tested, brushing occasionally with sauce. Discard bay leaf and serve sauce on the side.
Makes: 10 to 12 servings

Shrimped Spaghetti

1   lb. spaghetti
⅓   cup olive oil
2   cups peeled cooked shrimp
1   clove garlic, minced
⅓   cup grated Parmesan cheese
¼   cup chopped fresh dill
1   tsp. COOKIES Flavor Enhancer

1. Prepare spaghetti according to package directions; drain and rinse. In a large skillet, heat oil; add shrimp and garlic. Stir and cook for 5 minutes. Add cooked spaghetti, Parmesan cheese, dill, and Flavor Enhancer. Toss well to coat spaghetti.
Makes: 6 servings

Shrimp & Rice

2   cups fresh or canned, peeled cooked shrimp
2   cups cooked rice
¼   cup sliced olives
2   cups COOKIES Taco Sauce & Dip
½   cup grated Parmesan cheese

1. Gently combine shrimp and rice in a small, covered casserole; top with olives. Pour Taco Sauce over rice mixture. Sprinkle with cheese. Bake in 350° oven for 20 minutes or until heated through.
Makes: 4 servings

Tuna Tacos

2   9-oz. cans tuna, drained and flaked
½   cup COOKIES Taco Sauce & Dip
½   tsp. garlic salt
4   taco shells
1   large tomato, chopped
1   cup shredded lettuce
1   cup shredded cheddar cheese
1   avocado, seeded, peeled, and chopped
¼   cup minced green onions

1. Combine tuna, Taco Sauce, and garlic salt. Heat taco shells as instructed on package. Divide tuna mixture among taco shells. Top with remaining ingredients.
Makes: 4 servings

South-of-the-Border Shrimp

½   cup diced onion
1   medium green sweet pepper, diced
½   cup diced celery
1   tbsp. butter
1   16-oz. can tomatoes
1   18-oz. bottle COOKIES Taco Sauce & Dip
1½ lbs. peeled cooked shrimp
3   cups hot cooked rice

1. Cook onion, green pepper, and celery in butter until tender; add tomatoes and Taco Sauce. Heat to boiling; reduce heat. Simmer, covered, for 30 minutes. Add shrimp and cook until heated through. Serve with rice.
Makes: 6 servings

SIDE DISHES

Chapter 6

Sweet Onions on the Grill

6   tsp. butter

6   medium onions, peeled and cored

6   tsp. COOKIES Flavor Enhancer

6   tsp. brown sugar

1   12-oz. can beer or nonalcoholic beer

1. Place 1 teaspoon butter into each cored onion. Sprinkle each onion with 1 teaspoon each of Flavor Enhancer and brown sugar. Place onions, cored sides up, in a foil pan. Pour beer around the bottom of the onions. Cover with foil. Arrange medium-hot coals around edges of grill; place pan in center of grill. Grill, covered, for 45 minutes. Let stand 5 minutes before serving.

Makes: 6 servings

the "SAUCEMAN" says

If you're boiling an onion, pierce it lengthwise with a skewer to keep it from falling apart.

Bar-B-Qued Carrots

1   lb. pkg. peeled baby carrots

2   tbsp. butter or margarine

Dash COOKIES Flavor Enhancer

½   cup COOKIES Original Bar-B-Q Sauce

1. Cook carrots, covered, in boiling, lightly salted water in a large skillet for 8 to 10 minutes or until just tender. Drain and cool slightly. Melt butter in same skillet; add carrots and cook over medium heat until lightly browned, stirring occasionally. Add Flavor Enhancer and Bar-B-Q Sauce. Heat through and serve.

Makes: 6 servings

Marinated Vegetables

1   16-oz. bottle Italian salad dressing

¼   cup soy sauce

1   large onion, thinly sliced

2   green, yellow, and/or red sweet peppers,
      cut into strips

8   oz. asparagus spears, trimmed

1   medium zucchini, sliced

6   green onions, trimmed

    COOKIES Flavor Enhancer

    Grated Parmesan cheese

1. In a resealable plastic bag, combine salad dressing and soy sauce; add vegetables. Seal bag and marinate overnight in refrigerator, turning bag occasionally. Drain vegetables and place in a grill basket. Cook directly over medium coals for 5 to 6 minutes or until vegetables are tender-crisp, turning basket once. Sprinkle with Flavor Enhancer and Parmesan cheese.
Makes: 6 servings

Stuffed Peppers

8   oz. ground beef

1   cup chopped mushrooms

½   cup chopped onion

½   cup chopped pitted ripe olives

1   egg, beaten

1½ cups soft bread crumbs

½   cup COOKIES Original Bar-B-Q Sauce

8   small green sweet peppers

1. Combine ground beef, mushrooms, onion, and olives; add egg and mix well. Add bread crumbs and Bar-B-Q Sauce; mix thoroughly. Cut the tops off the peppers. Remove seeds and membranes. Fill peppers with the meat mixture. Place peppers in a baking dish. Pour ½ cup water in the bottom of the baking dish. Bake, covered, in a 350° oven for 1½ hours.
Makes: 8 servings

the "SAUCEMAN" says

Save the heels from all your bread, plus any stale bread, in plastic bags in the freezer. Make crumbs by chopping frozen slices in a blender or food processor when needed.

Cajun Green Beans

3   14½-oz. cans cut green beans, drained

1   8-oz. can sliced water chestnuts, drained

1   onion, finely chopped

½   cup COOKIES Original Bar-B-Q Sauce

½   cup COOKIES Western Style Bar-B-Q Sauce

6   slices bacon, crisp-cooked and crumbled

1   tsp. COOKIES Flavor Enhancer

1. In a 1½-quart casserole, combine beans, water chestnuts, onion, Bar-B-Q Sauces, bacon, and Flavor Enhancer. Bake, covered, in a 375° oven for 45 to 60 minutes or until done.

Makes: 8 servings

Steamed Cabbage on the Grill

1   large head cabbage

¾   cup beer or nonalcoholic beer

¼   cup butter, melted

2   tbsp. COOKIES Flavor Enhancer

1. Core cabbage. Place cabbage, cored side up, on a large piece of heavy duty foil. Combine beer, butter, and Flavor Enhancer. Pour beer mixture in the core and wrap cabbage in the foil. Arrange medium hot coals around the center of the grill; place wrapped cabbage in center of grill. Grill, covered, for 45 minutes. Unwrap cabbage; slice and serve.

Makes: 6 to 8 servings

Grilled Corn on the Husk

4   ears fresh corn on the cob

2   tsp. corn oil

2   tsp. chopped fresh herbs, such as thyme, marjoram, savory, and/or chives

     COOKIES Flavor Enhancer, to taste

1. Gently pull the husks back from corn but do not detach them. Pull off and discard the corn silk, then return the husks to their original positions, covering the ears. Soak the corn in water to cover for 30 minutes. Grill corn directly over medium coals for 25 to 30 minutes, turning occasionally. Discard the husks and brush corn with oil. Sprinkle with herbs and Flavor Enhancer.

Makes: 4 servings

the "SAUCEMAN" says

To remove every strand of silk from corn on the cob, dampen a paper towel or terry cloth and brush downward.

Marinated Cucumbers

½   cup vinegar

¼   cup sugar

1   tsp. salt

6   cups peeled and sliced cucumbers

1   large onion, chopped

1. In a covered container, combine vinegar, sugar, and salt. Add cucumbers and onion; toss to coat. Cover and chill for at least 4 hours or up to 5 days, stirring occasionally.

Makes: 12 servings

Potatoes & Assorted Vegetables on the Grill

6	medium potatoes, sliced
1	green sweet pepper, chopped
1	large onion, chopped
¼	cup butter
1	tsp. COOKIES Flavor Enhancer
½	cup beer or nonalcoholic beer

1. Tear off a 36×18-inch piece of heavy duty foil; fold in half to make an 18-inch square. Place potatoes, green pepper, and onion in center of foil. Dot with butter and sprinkle with Flavor Enhancer. Carefully pour on beer. Bring up opposite edges of foil and seal with a double fold. Fold remaining edges together to completely enclose vegetables, leaving space for steam to build. Grill directly over medium coals for 45 minutes or until done, turning packet occasionally.
Makes: 6 to 8 servings

the "SAUCEMAN" says

Line the crisper section of your refrigerator with newspaper and wrap vegetables in it. Moisture will be absorbed and your veggies will stay fresher longer.

Marinated Carrot Salad

4	cups packaged peeled baby carrots
1	large green sweet pepper, cut into strips
1	lb. sweet onions, cut into thin wedges
¾	cup sugar
½	cup white vinegar
¼	cup salad oil
1	10¾-oz. can condensed tomato soup
½	cup COOKIES Taco Sauce & Dip
¼	tsp. COOKIES Flavor Enhancer

1. Cook carrots in a medium saucepan in boiling, lightly salted water for 8 to 10 minutes or until just tender. Drain; transfer to a large bowl. Add green pepper and onions. Heat sugar, vinegar, and oil in a pan over low heat until sugar is dissolved. Stir in soup, Taco Sauce, and Flavor Enhancer until smooth. Pour over vegetables and mix well. Cover and chill for 24 hours.
Makes: 12 servings

Honey-Glazed Carrots

10 to 12 small young carrots, washed
      and trimmed
2   tbsp. margarine or butter, melted
1   tbsp. packed brown sugar
1   tbsp. honey
2   tbsp. finely chopped fresh parsley

1. Cook carrots in boiling, lightly salted water in a large skillet for 10 to 15 minutes or until just tender. Drain. Add margarine, sugar, and honey to skillet; cook over low heat, turning frequently, until carrots are glazed. Before serving, sprinkle carrots with parsley.
Makes: 4 servings

Peacock Vegetables

2   medium red onions, cut into thin wedges
2   small yellow summer squash,
      cut into ½-inch slices
2   small zucchini, cut into ½-inch slices
3   red, yellow, and/or green sweet peppers,
      cut into ½-inch strips
4   cloves garlic, thinly sliced
2   tbsp. snipped fresh parsley
2   tbsp. balsamic vinegar
1   tbsp. olive oil
1   tsp. dried oregano, crushed
½   tsp. salt
¼   tsp. black pepper

1. In a 13×9×2-inch baking pan, combine vegetables and garlic. In a screw-top jar, combine parsley, vinegar, olive oil, oregano, salt, and pepper. Cover the jar tightly and shake well. Pour over the vegetables and toss to coat. Bake, uncovered, in a 425° oven for 25 minutes or until vegetables are tender-crisp, stirring twice.
Makes: 8 servings

Calico Beans

1½   lbs. ground beef
2   tbsp. finely chopped onion
1   large can pork and beans
1   16-oz. can red kidney beans, rinsed
     and drained
1   15-oz. can butter beans, rinsed and drained
¾   cup packed brown sugar
⅔   cup COOKIES Original Bar-B-Q Sauce
¼   cup ketchup
3   tbsp. Miracle Whip
2   tbsp. spicy mustard
½   lb. bacon, crisp-cooked and crumbled

1. Cook ground beef and onion in an extra large oven-proof skillet until meat is brown; drain fat. Stir in undrained pork and beans, kidney beans, butter beans, brown sugar, Bar-B-Q Sauce, ketchup, Miracle Whip, mustard, and bacon. Bake, covered, in a 300° oven for 1½ to 2 hours.

Makes: 4 to 6 servings

COOKIES Bean Casserole

½   lb. ground beef
1   cup finely chopped onion
½   lb. bacon
1   can kidney beans, rinsed and drained
1   can pork and beans, rinsed and drained
1   tbsp. yellow mustard
1   can butter beans, rinsed and drained
2   cups COOKIES Original Bar-B-Q Sauce

1. Brown ground beef and onion in a skillet; drain fat and put aside. Brown bacon until just done; drain fat. Mix the ground beef mixture, bacon, and remaining ingredients in a large casserole. Bake in a 350° oven for 1 hour.

Makes: 4 to 6 servings

Prick bacon thoroughly with a fork as it fries and it will lie flat in the pan.

COOKIES Quick-Style Beans

1   28-oz. can oven-style baked beans, drained
½   cup COOKIES Western Style Bar-B-Q Sauce
¼   cup packed brown sugar
1   tbsp. COOKIES Flavor Enhancer
½   cup finely chopped onion (optional)
4   slices bacon, crisp-cooked and crumbled
     (optional)

1. In a large saucepan, combine the beans, Bar-B-Q Sauce, brown sugar, Flavor Enhancer, and, if desired, onion. Cook, stirring occasionally, over medium heat until heated through. If desired, stir in bacon.
Makes: 6 servings

Variety Baked Beans

1   lb. ground beef
1   lb. bacon, crisp-cooked and crumbled
1   16-oz. can pork and beans
1   16-oz. can kidney beans, rinsed and drained
1   15-oz. can green lima beans, rinsed
     and drained
1   15-oz. can butter beans, rinsed and drained
2   green sweet peppers, chopped
1   onion, finely chopped
1   cup COOKIES Original Bar-B-Q Sauce
¼   cup COOKIES Country Blend Bar-B-Q Sauce
1   Anaheim chile pepper, chopped
4   cloves garlic, minced

1. Cook ground beef in a large skillet; drain fat. Combine all ingredients in a 2½- to 3-quart casserole. Bake, covered, in a 400° oven for 1 hour.
Makes: 10 to 12 servings

COOKIES Spanish Rice Peppers

1   cup long grain rice

4   medium green sweet peppers

⅔   cup COOKIES Original Bar-B-Q Sauce

12   oz. American cheese, shredded

1. Cook rice according to package directions. Halve peppers lengthwise, removing seeds and membranes. Cook peppers in boiling, lightly salted water for 5 minutes; drain. Combine rice, Bar-B-Q Sauce, and 1 cup of the cheese. Place pepper halves, cut side up, in a 2-quart baking dish. Spoon rice mixture into peppers. Bake, covered, in a 350° oven for 20 minutes. Sprinkle with remaining cheese and bake for 5 minutes more or until heated through.
Makes: 4 servings

Eggplant Delight

1   medium eggplant

¾   cup water

1   small onion, diced

1   tbsp. butter

¼   cup COOKIES Taco Sauce & Dip

½   cup grated Parmesan cheese

¼   cup bacon bits

2   tbsp. chopped fresh parsley

1   5-oz. can evaporated milk

¾   cup cracker crumbs

3   tbsp. butter, melted

1. Peel and dice eggplant. In a large saucepan, combine eggplant and water. Bring to boiling; reduce heat. Simmer, covered, 15 minutes; drain in colander. In the same pan, cook onion in 1 tablespoon butter until tender. Stir in eggplant, Taco Sauce, Parmesan cheese, bacon bits, and parsley. Transfer to a 1½-quart casserole. Pour evaporated milk over mixture. Stir gently. Mix cracker crumbs and melted butter. Sprinkle over eggplant mixture. Bake in a 375° oven for 30 minutes or until heated through.
Makes: 4 servings

the "SAUCEMAN" says

When making cracker crumbs, put crackers in a clear bag and crush them with a rolling pin. You'll have no mess, and you can easily pour the crumbs into a measuring cup.

Corn Risotto

1   cup chopped onion

2   tbsp. butter

1   cup COOKIES Taco Sauce & Dip

2   cups shredded Swiss cheese

1   15-oz. can cream-style corn

1   16-oz. pkg. frozen broccoli cuts,
      cooked and drained

½   cup crushed corn chips

1. In a medium saucepan, cook onion in butter until tender. Add Taco Sauce. Remove from heat; stir in cheese and corn. Stir to melt the cheese. Add broccoli; place in a 2-quart casserole dish. Sprinkle with corn chips. Bake, uncovered, in a 350° oven for 30 minutes or until heated through.
Makes: 4 to 6 servings

Potatoes Supreme

2   lbs. frozen hash brown potatoes, thawed

1   tsp. COOKIES Flavor Enhancer

2   cups shredded cheddar cheese

1   10¾-oz. can condensed cream of chicken soup

1   cup milk

1   8-oz. carton dairy sour cream

2   tbsp. chopped onion

2   cups crushed cornflakes

½   cup butter, melted

1. Place thawed hash browns in a 13×9×2-inch baking pan. Sprinkle with Flavor Enhancer. Combine cheese, soup, milk, sour cream, and onion; spoon on top of potatoes. Top with cornflakes and drizzle with melted butter. Bake, uncovered, in a 350° oven for 1 hour.
Makes: 16 servings

Heavenly Onions

4 large Bermuda onions, sliced and
   separated into rings
¼ cup butter
½ lb. Swiss cheese
1 10¾-oz. can condensed cream of chicken soup
½ cup milk or cooking sherry
1 tsp. soy sauce
¼ tsp. COOKIES Flavor Enhancer
1 to 2 tbsp. butter, softened
8 thin slices French bread

1. In a large skillet, cook onions in ¼ cup butter until tender. Place in a greased 2-quart baking dish. Top with cheese. Combine soup, milk, soy sauce, and Flavor Enhancer in a saucepan; heat through. Pour over cheese. Spread softened butter on one side of bread slices; overlap bread in a ring around the outside edge of the dish, butter side up. Bake, uncovered, in a 350° oven for 30 minutes.
Makes: 6 servings

Zucchini Delight

1 cup packaged biscuit mix
1 cup COOKIES Taco Sauce & Dip
4 eggs, beaten
½ cup grated Parmesan cheese
½ cup diced onion
¼ cup vegetable oil
2 tbsp. chopped fresh parsley
½ tsp. dried oregano, crushed
½ tsp. COOKIES Flavor Enhancer
1 clove garlic, minced
3 cups shredded zucchini

1. Mix all ingredients except zucchini. Gently fold in zucchini. Spread evenly in a lightly greased 13×9×2-inch baking pan. Bake, uncovered, in a 350° oven for 45 minutes or until done. Cut into small squares and serve warm.
Makes: 12 servings

Slow-Cooked Potatoes

Nonstick cooking spray
1 12-oz. pkg. frozen hash brown potatoes
1 10¾-oz. can condensed cream of potato soup
1 soup can full of milk
1 tbsp. butter, melted
½ tsp. COOKIES Flavor Enhancer
1 cup shredded cheddar cheese

1. Lightly coat a 3½- or 4-quart slow cooker with cooking spray. Add potatoes, soup, milk, butter, and Flavor Enhancer. Cook, covered, on low-heat setting for 4 to 5 hours. Sprinkle with cheese before serving.
Makes: 4 to 5 servings

Sweet Potato Casserole

1 24-oz. can sweet potatoes
½ cup granulated sugar
⅓ cup butter or margarine, melted
¼ cup evaporated milk
2 eggs, beaten
1 tbsp. vanilla
1 cup shredded or flaked coconut
⅓ cup all-purpose flour
⅓ cup butter or margarine, melted
¼ cup packed brown sugar
1 cup pecans, chopped

1. Combine sweet potatoes, granulated sugar, ⅓ cup melted butter, evaporated milk, eggs, and vanilla; transfer to a 2-quart baking dish. Combine coconut, flour, ⅓ cup butter, brown sugar, and pecans; spoon over top of potato mixture. Bake, uncovered, in a 350° oven for 30 to 40 minutes or until center is set.
Makes: 6 to 8 servings

Mexico in a Pan

12	flour tortillas
½	cup vegetable oil
½	cup chopped green onion
1½	cups COOKIES Taco Sauce & Dip
1	cup shredded Monterey Jack cheese
½	tsp. COOKIES Flavor Enhancer
½	tsp. dried oregano
1	8-oz. carton dairy sour cream

1. Cut tortillas into thin strips. Heat oil in a skillet. Cook onions and tortilla strips, turning occasionally, for 10 minutes or until crisp; drain oil. Stir in Taco Sauce, cheese, Flavor Enhancer, and oregano. Heat until cheese is melted. Top with sour cream.
Makes: 4 to 6 servings

Spinach Enchiladas

4	green onions, chopped
1	tbsp. margarine
2	10-oz. pkgs. frozen chopped spinach, thawed and drained
2	cups shredded cheddar cheese
1	8-oz. carton dairy sour cream
1	18-oz. bottle COOKIES Taco Sauce & Dip
10	7- to 8-inch flour tortillas

1. Cook green onions in margarine in a large skillet. Add spinach and cook for 2 minutes. Remove from heat and stir in 1½ cups of the cheese, sour cream, and 1 cup of the Taco Sauce. Divide mixture equally among tortillas. Roll up and place, seam side down, in a 3-quart baking dish. Pour on remaining Taco Sauce; sprinkle with remaining ½ cup cheese. Bake, uncovered, in a 350° oven for 35 minutes or until heated through.
Makes: 4 to 6 servings

Cheesy Bar-B-Q Potato Bake

1 10¾-oz. can condensed cheddar cheese soup
½ cup COOKIES Original Bar-B-Q Sauce
⅓ cup evaporated milk
1 tbsp. finely chopped onion
½ tsp. COOKIES Flavor Enhancer
4 medium potatoes, peeled and sliced
1 cup shredded cheddar cheese

1. In a bowl, combine soup, Bar-B-Q Sauce, evaporated milk, onion, and Flavor Enhancer. Grease the bottom of a 2-quart baking dish. Layer one-third of the potatoes in the dish. Top with half of the soup mixture. Repeat with potatoes and soup mixture, ending with a layer of potatoes. Sprinkle cheese over top layer of potatoes. Bake, covered, in a 375° oven for 1¼ hours or until potatoes are tender.
Makes: 4 to 6 servings

Potato Skins

4 large potatoes
2 tsp. margarine or butter, melted
1 cup shredded Colby and Monterey Jack cheese
½ cup dairy sour cream
½ cup sliced green onions
½ cup COOKIES Premium Salsa
   COOKIES Wings-N-Things Hot Sauce
   (optional)

1. Scrub potatoes; pierce with a fork. Bake in a 425° oven for 40 to 60 minutes or until tender. Let stand until cool enough to handle. Cut each potato lengthwise into four wedges. Scoop out pulp of potato, leaving a ¼-inch-thick shell. Refrigerate pulp to use for another purpose. Place potato skins on broiler pan, skin side down; brush with melted margarine. Broil 4 to 5 inches from heat for 8 to 10 minutes or until lightly browned. Sprinkle with cheese and broil for 30 seconds.

2. Serve hot with sour cream, green onions, and Salsa, or, if desired, drizzle Wings-N-Things over them for a spicy treat.
Makes: 4 servings

Rice Pilaf

¼　cup chopped onion

2　tbsp. margarine or butter

1　cup uncooked regular or long grain rice

2¼　cups chicken broth

¼　tsp. salt

1. Cook onion in margarine in a medium saucepan until tender. Stir in rice; cook and stir for 5 minutes. Add broth and salt. Bring to boiling; reduce heat. Simmer, covered, for 16 minutes. Let stand, covered, for 5 minutes.
Makes: 4 servings

Southwestern-Style Rice

1　14-oz. can chicken broth

½　cup water

½　cup **COOKIES Premium Salsa**

2　cups uncooked instant rice

1. Heat broth, water, and Salsa to a boil in a medium saucepan. Stir in rice. Cover and remove from heat. Let stand for 5 minutes. Fluff with a fork.
Makes: 4 servings

COOKIES Yams

4 medium yams or sweet potatoes
½ cup butter
¼ tsp. COOKIES Flavor Enhancer
1½ cups COOKIES Original Bar-B-Q Sauce

1. Scrub potatoes; prick with a fork. Bake in a 425° oven for 40 to 60 minutes or until tender; cool and peel. Cut in half lengthwise and arrange in a 2-quart rectangular baking dish. Dot with chunks of butter. Sprinkle with Flavor Enhancer. Pour Bar-B-Q Sauce over the top. Bake, covered, in a 350° oven for 15 to 20 minutes or until heated through.

Makes: 4 servings

the "SAUCEMAN" says

Select small- or medium-sized sweet potatoes free of cracks or damp areas. Look for potatoes that are tapered at both ends.

Zesty Mac & Cheese

1 box macaroni and cheese dinner mix
1½ cups COOKIES Taco Sauce & Dip
1 cup shredded cheddar cheese
½ cup shredded Swiss cheese
½ cup crushed corn chips

1. Prepare macaroni and cheese dinner according to package directions. Stir in Taco Sauce, ½ cup of the cheddar cheese, and the Swiss cheese. Pour into a greased 1½-quart casserole. Top with remaining ½ cup cheddar cheese and corn chips. Bake, uncovered, in a 350° oven for 30 minutes or until heated through.

Makes: 4 servings

Corn Casserole

2   eggs

1   8-oz. carton dairy sour cream

½   cup margarine, melted

1   pkg. corn bread mix

1   15-oz. can whole kernel corn, drained

1   15-oz. can cream-style corn

1. Beat eggs well. Add sour cream, margarine, and corn bread mix; stir well. Fold in drained corn and cream-style corn. Grease a 2-quart baking dish. Pour mixture into dish. Bake, uncovered, in a 350° oven for 30 minutes or until set.
Makes: 6 to 8 servings

Scalloped Corn

1   15-oz. can whole kernel corn, drained

1   15-oz. can cream-style corn

¾   cup crushed soda crackers

⅔   cup milk

1   egg, beaten

1   tbsp. butter

1. Combine corns, ½ cup of the crackers, milk, and egg; pour into a 1½-quart casserole. Sprinkle with remaining ¼ cup crackers and dot with butter. Bake in a 350° oven for 45 minutes or until set.
Makes: 6 servings

Hot Potato

4	large baking potatoes
¼	lb. ground beef
2	tbsp. COOKIES Taco Sauce & Dip
1	3½-oz. can chopped ripe olives
2	chopped green chiles
2	tbsp. finely chopped onion
1	cup shredded cheddar cheese
1	8-oz. carton dairy sour cream
	COOKIES Flavor Enhancer

1. Scrub potatoes; pierce with a fork. Wrap each potato in foil. Bake in a 350° oven for 70 to 80 minutes or until tender; discard foil. Meanwhile, brown ground beef in a small skillet; drain fat and add 1 tablespoon Taco Sauce. Set aside. When potatoes are done, let cool until they can be handled. Halve potatoes lengthwise; scoop pulp out of each potato. Mash potato pulp with remaining tablespoon of Taco Sauce. Spoon into potato shells. Sprinkle with ground beef, olives, chiles, onion, and cheese. Bake in a 300° oven for 25 to 30 minutes or until heated through. Top with sour cream and Flavor Enhancer.

Makes: 4 servings

Potatoes soaked in salt water for 20 minutes will bake more rapidly.

Pineapple-Cheese Casserole

1	20-oz. can pineapple chunks or tidbits
1	cup shredded cheddar cheese
¾	cup sugar
1	tbsp. all-purpose flour
1	cup soft bread crumbs
	Butter

1. Drain pineapple, reserving juice. Place drained pineapple and cheese in a 2-quart square baking dish. Combine reserved juice, sugar, and flour; cook and stir until mixture comes to a boil. Pour liquid over pineapple in dish. Top with bread crumbs and dot with butter. Bake, covered, in a 350° oven for 30 minutes. Uncover and bake for 10 minutes more or until crumbs are lightly browned. Serve warm.

Makes: 4 to 6 servings

Bacon Corn Bread

Nonstick cooking spray

2 **cups yellow cornmeal**

2 **cups all-purpose flour**

2 **tbsp. baking powder**

2 **tsp. COOKIES Flavor Enhancer**

2½ **cups milk**

½ **cup butter, melted**

2 **eggs, beaten**

½ **cup real bacon bits**

1. Lightly coat a 13×9×2-inch baking pan with cooking spray. In a large bowl, combine all ingredients; mix well. Put into prepared pan. Bake in a 425° oven for 30 to 35 minutes or until a toothpick inserted near center comes out clean. Cut into squares and serve warm.

Makes: 16 servings

Zucchini Pancakes

4 **to 5 medium zucchini**
   (about 1½ lbs.), shredded

2 **eggs**

¾ **cup all-purpose flour**

¼ **cup grated Parmesan cheese**

1 **tbsp. finely chopped onion**

½ **tsp. COOKIES Flavor Enhancer**

¼ **tsp. garlic powder**

   Cooking oil

   COOKIES Flavor Enhancer

1. Thoroughly drain zucchini in a colander, gently pressing occasionally. Pat dry with paper towels. Measure 5 cups well-drained zucchini; set aside. Beat eggs in a mixing bowl. Stir in flour, Parmesan cheese, onion, ½ teaspoon Flavor Enhancer, and garlic powder (batter will be lumpy). Stir in zucchini just until moistened.

2. Lightly oil a griddle; heat over medium-low heat. Add batter by the tablespoon, spreading each to a 4-inch circle. Cook for 1½ to 2 minutes on each side or until golden brown. Season with additional Flavor Enhancer.

Makes: 8 servings

DESSERTS

Chapter 7

Butterscotch Pie

1½ cups packed light brown sugar

3 tbsp. cornstarch

2 tbsp. all-purpose flour

¼ tsp. salt

1½ cups water

2 egg yolks

1 tbsp. butter

1 tsp. vanilla

1 baked 9-inch pastry shell

Your favorite meringue recipe

1. Combine brown sugar, cornstarch, flour, and salt in a medium saucepan. Add water and stir well. Cook and stir over medium heat until mixture thickens and clears. Beat yolks. Gradually stir 1 cup hot mixture into yolks. Slowly blend yolk mixture back to saucepan, stirring constantly. Cook and stir over low heat for 1 minute. Remove from heat and stir in butter and vanilla. Pour into pastry shell. Top hot filling with meringue, sealing to edge. Bake in a 325° oven for 30 minutes.
Makes: 8 servings

Caramel Apple Pizza

1 20-oz. pkg. refrigerated sugar cookie dough

2 8-oz. pkgs. fat-free cream cheese, softened

1 cup packed brown sugar

1 tsp. vanilla

5 medium apples

½ cup water

1 tbsp. lemon juice

¼ cup fat-free caramel ice cream topping

1. Pat cookie dough over the bottom of an ungreased deep-dish pizza pan. Bake in a 350° oven for 11 to 14 minutes or until light brown. Let stand until cool. Combine cream cheese, brown sugar, and vanilla in a bowl. Beat until smooth. Spread over cooled cookie crust. Peel, core, and slice apples. Dip slices into a mixture of water and lemon juice to prevent browning. Arrange slices on the cream cheese mixture; drizzle caramel topping over the top. Cut into wedges with pizza cutter to serve.
Makes: 10 to 12 servings

the "SAUCEMAN" says

To create inexpensive fruit-flavored syrup, add 2 cups sugar to 1 cup of any kind of fruit and cook until it boils.

Cheesecake

1½   cups graham cracker crumbs

2   tbsp. sugar

½   cup margarine, melted

1   8-oz. pkg. cream cheese, softened

1   cup sugar

1   3-oz. pkg. lemon-flavored gelatin

⅔   cup boiling water

½   cup cold water

1   12-oz. can evaporated milk, very cold
     Graham cracker crumbs

1. Combine graham cracker crumbs, 2 tablespoons sugar, and margarine. Press into 13×9×2-inch baking pan. Beat together cream cheese and 1 cup sugar. Dissolve gelatin in boiling water. Stir in cold water and chill until gelatin is as thick as egg whites. Pour cold evaporated milk into a chilled bowl. Whip as for whipping cream. Gradually beat in thickened gelatin mixture. Add cream cheese mixture, stirring until combined. Pour into crumb-lined pan. Garnish with extra graham cracker crumbs. Chill until firm.
Makes: 12 servings

Pecan Pie

1   cup sugar

1   cup light-color corn syrup

3   eggs, well beaten

1   tbsp. butter, melted

1¼   cups pecans, chopped

1   unbaked 9-inch pastry shell

1. Thoroughly mix sugar, corn syrup, eggs, and butter; add pecans and mix. Pour into pastry shell. Bake in a 350° oven for 1¼ hours. Cool on a wire rack.
Makes: 8 servings

Grasshopper Pie

32 large marshmallows
½   cup milk
¼   cup crème de menthe
2   tbsp. white crème de cacao
    Few drops green food coloring
1   cup whipping cream
1   chocolate-flavored crumb pie shell
    Chocolate curls

1. In a saucepan, heat marshmallows and milk over low heat, stirring constantly, until marshmallows are melted; let cool. Stir in liqueurs and food coloring. Whip cream in small bowl until stiff. Fold whipped cream into cooled marshmallow mixture. Blend thoroughly. Spoon into pie shell. Chill for 3 to 4 hours. Garnish with chocolate curls.
Makes: 8 servings

Straw-Rhubarb Pie

    Pastry for double-crust pie
5   cups rhubarb
1½ cups sugar
⅓   cup wild strawberry-flavored gelatin
¼   cup all-purpose flour

1. Roll out half the pastry on floured surface and fit into a 9-inch pie plate; set aside. Mix rhubarb, sugar, gelatin, and flour and pour into pastry shell. Trim pastry to edge of pie plate. Roll out remaining pastry and place on top of rhubarb mixture. Trim edges, fold top crust under bottom crust, and flute edges. Cut slits in top crust to allow steam to escape. Bake in a 400° oven for 15 minutes; reduce temperature to 375° and bake for 35 to 45 minutes more until golden brown.
Makes: 8 servings

the "SAUCEMAN" says

Give a unique look to your pies by using a fluted pastry wheel to cut the dough.

Peanut Butter Pie

1   cup corn syrup

1   cup sugar

3   eggs, slightly beaten

⅓   cup peanut butter

½   tsp. vanilla

1   unbaked 9-inch pastry shell

1. Mix syrup, sugar, eggs, peanut butter, and vanilla. Pour into pastry shell. Bake in a 350° oven for 45 minutes. Cool on a wire rack.

Makes: 8 servings

Raisin Pie

2   cups raisins

2¼   cups water

½   cup packed brown sugar

2   tbsp. cornstarch

½   tsp. ground cinnamon

⅛   tsp. salt

1½   tbsp. butter

1   tbsp. vinegar

1   unbaked 9-inch pastry shell

1. Combine raisins and 2 cups of the water in a medium saucepan. Heat to boiling; remove from heat. Cover and let stand for 30 minutes. Stir together brown sugar, cornstarch, cinnamon, salt, and the remaining ¼ cup water; stir into raisin mixture. Cook and stir until thickened and bubbly; remove from heat. Add butter and vinegar. Transfer to pastry shell. Bake in a 450° oven for 10 minutes; reduce temperature to 375° and bake another 35 to 40 minutes.

Makes: 8 servings

Pumpkin Pie Crunch

1 15-oz. can pumpkin
1 12-oz. can evaporated milk
3 eggs
1½ cups sugar
4 tsp. pumpkin pie spice
½ tsp. salt
1 2-layer yellow cake mix
1 cup pecans, chopped
1 cup butter or margarine, melted
   Whipped dessert topping

1. Grease a 13×9×2-inch baking pan. Combine pumpkin, evaporated milk, eggs, sugar, pumpkin pie spice, and salt in a large bowl; pour into pan. Sprinkle dry cake mix evenly over pumpkin mixture. Top with pecans. Drizzle with melted butter. Bake in a 350° oven for 50 to 55 minutes or until top is golden. Cool completely before serving. Top with whipped topping. Chill leftovers.
Makes: 12 to 16 servings

Quick Cherry Pie

1 3-oz. pkg. cherry-flavored gelatin
1 cup boiling water
1 21-oz. can cherry pie filling
1 baked 9-inch pastry shell
   Whipped dessert topping
   Chopped toasted pecans (optional)

1. Dissolve gelatin in boiling water; add pie filling. After mixture thickens, pour into pastry shell. Chill in refrigerator until set. Serve with whipped dessert topping. If desired, garnish with pecans.
Makes: 8 servings

Easy Apple Pie

Pastry for double-crust pie
1 cup sugar
1 tsp. ground cinnamon
½ tsp. ground nutmeg
6 cups thinly sliced peeled apples
1 tbsp. butter

1. Place 1 pie crust in bottom of 9-inch pie pan. Combine sugar, cinnamon, and nutmeg; mix with apples. Arrange in pie; dot with butter. Trim pastry to edge of pie pan. Top with second crust; trim, seal, and flute edges. Cut slits in top crust to allow steam to escape. Bake in a 450° oven for 10 minutes; reduce temperature to 350° and bake another 40 minutes.
Makes: 8 servings

Mock Apple Pie

3 cups all-purpose flour
3 tbsp. sugar
1 tsp. salt
1¼ cups shortening
1 egg
5 tbsp. water
2 cups water
1½ cups sugar
2 tsp. cream of tartar
22 whole Ritz crackers
1 tsp. ground cinnamon
Juice of 1 lemon

1. For crust, mix flour, 3 tablespoons sugar, and salt. Cut in shortening with a pastry blender or 2 forks until mixture resembles coarse crumbs. Add egg and 5 tablespoons water; stir until moistened. Shape into a ball. Wrap and chill in refrigerator for 1 hour.

2. Roll out half the dough on a floured board. Transfer to a 9-inch pie plate. For filling, combine 2 cups water, 1½ cups sugar, and cream of tartar; bring to a boil. Add crackers and boil for 90 seconds. Pour mixture into unbaked pie shell. Sprinkle with cinnamon and lemon juice. Roll out remaining pastry and place on top of filling; trim, seal, and flute edges. Cut slits in top crust to allow steam to escape. Bake in a 450° oven for 15 minutes.
Makes: 8 servings

Layered Coconut-Pecan Delight

1½   cups all-purpose flour
1   cup chopped pecans
½   cup butter, melted
2⅔   cups coconut
1   8-oz. pkg. cream cheese, softened
3   cups cold milk
1   pkg. instant vanilla pudding
1   8-oz. carton whipped dessert topping

1. Combine flour, ½ cup of the pecans, and butter. Press into 13×9×2-inch baking dish. Bake in a 350° oven for 15 minutes; let cool. Reduce oven temperature to 325°. Spread remaining ½ cup pecans and ⅔ cup of the coconut on baking sheet; bake for 5 minutes or until toasted. Beat cream cheese until very soft. Gradually add ½ cup of the milk and blend until smooth. Add remaining 2½ cups milk and pudding mix. Beat with an electric mixer on low speed about 2 minutes. Stir in remaining 2 cups coconut and pour immediately over baked crust. Spread whipped dessert topping over pudding mixture. Sprinkle with toasted coconut and pecans. Cover and chill 2 hours.
Makes: 12 to 15 servings

Rhubarb Torte

1   cup all-purpose flour
2   tbsp. sugar
    Dash salt
½   cup butter
2¼   cup chopped rhubarb
1½   cups sugar
⅓   cup sour cream
¼   cup all-purpose flour
3   egg yolks, beaten
    Meringue

1. For crust, mix 1 cup flour, 2 tablespoons sugar, and salt; cut in butter with a pastry cutter until mixture is crumbly. Pat into 9×9×2-inch baking pan. Bake in a 350° oven for 25 minutes.

2. Combine rhubarb, 1½ cups sugar, sour cream, ¼ cup flour, and egg yolks in a saucepan and cook until thick; spread over crust. Spread meringue over rhubarb filling; seal to edge. Bake 15 minutes; cool.
Makes: 9 servings

Meringue: In a large bowl, beat 3 egg whites and ¼ teaspoon cream of tartar until soft peaks form. Gradually add 6 tablespoons sugar, beating on high speed until mixture forms stiff, glossy peaks and sugar dissolves.

Chocolate Brownie Cobbler

2   cups unsalted butter

1⅔   cups semisweet chocolate chips

4   cups sugar

8   large eggs

1   tsp. vanilla

1⅔   cups all-purpose flour

1   tsp. salt

2½   cups coarsely chopped walnuts

      Cocoa powder (optional)

      Vanilla ice cream, premium type

1. Butter a 15×10×2-inch baking dish. Stir butter and chocolate chips in a heavy saucepan over low to medium heat until melted and smooth. Remove pan from heat. Whisk sugar into the chocolate mixture. Whisk in eggs, 1 at a time. Whisk in vanilla, then flour and salt. Stir in walnuts. Transfer batter to prepared baking dish.

2. Bake in a 350° oven for about 50 minutes until top is crisp and tester comes out with wet crumbs attached. Cool for 15 minutes. If desired, dust with cocoa powder. Spoon warm cobbler into bowls. Serve with vanilla ice cream.

Makes: 15 servings

Peach Cobbler

½   cup sugar

1   tbsp. cornstarch

¼   tsp. ground cinnamon

4   cups sliced, peeled, and pitted peaches

1   tsp. lemon juice

1   cup all-purpose flour

1   tbsp. sugar

1½   tsp. baking powder

½   tsp. salt

3   tbsp. shortening

½   cup milk

1. Mix ½ cup sugar, cornstarch, and cinnamon in a saucepan. Stir in peaches and lemon juice. Cook, stirring constantly, until mixture thickens and boils. Cook and stir for 1 minute more. Pour into an ungreased 1½-quart casserole. Put peach mixture in oven to keep hot.

2. For topping, stir together flour, 1 tablespoon sugar, baking powder, and salt; cut in shortening until mixture resembles coarse crumbs. Stir in milk. Drop dough by spoon onto hot peach mixture. Bake in a 400° oven for 25 to 30 minutes or until top is golden brown.

Makes: 8 servings

Bread Pudding

4   eggs
½   cup sugar
1   tsp. vanilla
¼   tsp. salt
½   cup raisins (optional)
5   slices white bread
2½   cups milk, scalded
     Ground cinnamon

1. Slightly beat eggs (do not overbeat); add sugar, vanilla, and salt. Mix well. If desired, stir in raisins. Crumble bread slices into a 9×9×2-inch baking pan. Stir scalded milk into egg mixture; pour over bread in pan. Sprinkle top with cinnamon. Bake in a 450° oven for 8 minutes; reduce heat to 425° and bake another 12 minutes or until a knife inserted in center comes out clean.
Makes: 9 servings

DeLite's Miniature Pecan Tarts

½   of an 8-oz. pkg. cream cheese, softened
⅔   cup butter
1¼   cups all-purpose flour
¾   cup packed brown sugar
⅔   cup chopped pecans
1   egg, beaten
1   tbsp. butter, melted
1   tsp. vanilla
     Dash salt

1. Stir together cream cheese, ⅔ cup butter, and flour until smooth. Shape into 24 balls. Press in ungreased miniature muffin cups to form small shells. Stir together remaining ingredients. Spoon into tart shells. Bake in a 325° oven for 25 to 30 minutes or until filling is just set. Let cool before removing from pan.
Makes: 24 miniature tarts

the "SAUCEMAN" says

Soften butter or margarine quickly by grating it.

Rhubarb Dessert

4   to 5 cups chopped rhubarb
½   cup granulated sugar
¾   cup packed brown sugar
3   tbsp. all-purpose flour
⅓   cup butter
¾   cup packed brown sugar
¾   cup quick oatmeal
¾   cup all-purpose flour
¼   tsp. baking soda
¼   tsp. baking powder

1. Place first 4 ingredients in a 13×9×2-inch cake pan; stir together. Melt butter and mix with remaining ingredients. Crumble on top. Bake in a 375° oven about 45 minutes or until the rhubarb mixture bubbles through the topping.
Makes: 8 to 10 servings

Apple Crisp

4   large apples, sliced
¾   cup packed brown sugar
½   cup all-purpose flour
½   cup quick oatmeal
⅓   cup margarine, softened
¾   tsp. ground nutmeg
¾   tsp. ground cinnamon
    Vanilla ice cream (optional)

1. Grease bottom and sides of an 8×8×2-inch baking pan; put apples in pan. Mix brown sugar, flour, oats, margarine, nutmeg, and cinnamon; sprinkle over apples. Bake, uncovered, in a 375° oven for 30 minutes or until apples are tender. Serve warm or cooled. If desired, top with vanilla ice cream.
Makes: 6 servings

Strawberry Shortcake

1   quart strawberries, sliced
½   cup sugar
½   cup all-purpose flour
2   tbsp. sugar
3   tsp. baking powder
1   tsp. salt
⅓   cup shortening
¾   cup milk
     Whipped cream

1. Mix strawberries and ½ cup sugar. Set aside for 1 hour. Mix flour, 2 tablespoons sugar, baking powder, and salt; cut in shortening until mixture resembles crumbs. Add milk. Drop by tablespoon on an ungreased cookie sheet. Bake in a 450° oven for 10 to 12 minutes. Split shortcakes. Fill with strawberries and replace tops. Top with more strawberries and whipped cream.
Makes: 8 servings

Better Than Sex Cake

1   2-layer German chocolate cake mix
1   can Eagle Brand sweetened condensed milk
½   of a 10-oz. jar butterscotch topping
½   of a 10-oz. jar caramel topping
½   of a 10-oz. jar chocolate fudge topping
1   8-oz. carton whipped dessert topping
2   Skor or Heath candy bars, crushed

1. Bake cake mix according to box directions and using a 13×9×2-inch cake pan. Let cake cool and poke holes in the top. Mix next 4 ingredients and pour over cake. Spread whipped dessert over cake. Sprinkle with candy bars; cover and refrigerate for up to 6 hours.
Makes: 12 servings

the "SAUCEMAN" says

Add a pinch of baking soda to cake icing to keep it moist and prevent cracking once it's on the cake.

Fuzzy Navel Cake

1   2-layer yellow cake mix
½   cup cooking oil
1   pkg. instant vanilla pudding mix
4   eggs
¾   cup peach schnapps
½   cup orange juice
½   tsp. orange extract
1   cup powdered sugar
¼   cup peach schnapps
2   tbsp. orange juice

1. Grease and lightly flour a 9½-inch fluted cake pan or 10-inch tube pan. Combine cake mix, oil, pudding mix, eggs, ¾ cup schnapps, ½ cup orange juice, and orange extract; blend well. Pour into pan. Bake in a 350° oven for 45 to 50 minutes or until cake springs back when lightly touched.

2. For glaze, stir together powdered sugar, ¼ cup peach schnapps, and 2 tablespoons orange juice (mixture will be thin). While cake is still warm in pan, poke holes in it with a toothpick or skewer. Pour mixture over cake. Allow cake to cool for at least 2 hours before removing from pan.

Makes: 16 servings

Hawaiian Wedding Cake

1   2-layer yellow cake mix
1   4-serving pkg. instant vanilla pudding mix
1¾   cups milk
1   8-oz. pkg. cream cheese, softened
1   20-oz. can crushed pineapple, well drained
1   8-oz. carton whipped dessert topping
1   cup flaked or shredded coconut
    Kiwi fruit, sliced
    Maraschino cherries

1. Bake cake mix according to box directions using a 13×9×2-inch baking pan. Cool. Beat together pudding mix, milk, and cream cheese until smooth. Spread on top of cooled cake. Fold pineapple into whipped topping. Spread on top of pudding mixture. Sprinkle coconut on top and decorate with kiwi and maraschino cherries. Cover and chill.

Makes: 16 servings

Angel Food Cake Dessert

1   angel food cake
2   pkg. instant vanilla pudding mix
2   cups cold milk
1   16-oz. carton sour cream
1   can of your favorite pie filling
    Whipped dessert topping

1. Tear angel food cake into pieces and place in bottom of a greased 13×9×2-inch cake pan. Beat pudding, milk, and sour cream until smooth; pour over cake. Cover and chill for 1 hour. Top with pie filling. Garnish with whipped topping. Cover and chill for 4 hours before serving.
Makes: 12 servings

the "SAUCEMAN" says

Cut an apple in half and place it in the container with a cake; this keeps the cake fresh several days longer.

Very Moist Carrot Cake

1   cup sifted cake flour
2   tbsp. cake flour
½   cup packed brown sugar
½   cup granulated sugar
½   tsp. baking powder
½   tsp. baking soda
½   tsp. salt
½   tsp. ground cinnamon
1½ cups finely shredded carrots
¾   cup cooking oil
2   eggs
1   tsp. vanilla
    Cream Cheese Frosting

1. Grease and flour a 13×9×2-inch cake pan. Combine flours, sugars, baking powder, baking soda, salt, and cinnamon in large bowl. Add carrots, oil, eggs, and 1 teaspoon vanilla, beating for 2 to 3 minutes on medium speed; pour into baking pan. Bake in a 325° oven for 40 minutes. Cool on a wire rack. Spread Cream Cheese Frosting over cooled cake.
Makes: 12 servings

Cream Cheese Frosting: Beat together one 3-ounce package softened cream cheese, ¼ cup softened butter, 1 teaspoon vanilla, and 1½ cups sifted powdered sugar.

Chocolate Chiffon Cake

¾ cup boiling water

½ cup unsweetened cocoa powder

1¾ cups sifted all-purpose flour

1¾ cups sugar

1½ tsp. baking soda

1 tsp. salt

½ cup cooking oil

7 egg yolks

2 tsp. vanilla

7 egg whites

½ tsp. cream of tartar

Chocolate Frosting

1. Combine water and cocoa until smooth; cool. Sift flour, sugar, baking soda, and salt together in a bowl. Make a well in the center and add oil, egg yolks, cooled cocoa mixture, and vanilla; beat until smooth. Combine egg whites and cream of tartar in another bowl and beat with clean beaters until very stiff. Pour egg yolk mixture in thin stream over entire surface of egg whites, gently cutting and folding in with rubber spatula until completely blended. Pour into an ungreased 10-inch tube pan.

2. Bake in a 325° oven about 1 hour or until top springs back when lightly touched. Invert and hang on funnel for 15 minutes. Remove from pan and cool on rack. Frost top and sides of cake with Chocolate Frosting.
Makes: 12 servings

Chocolate Frosting: Beat two 3-ounce packages softened cream cheese with 3 tablespoons milk. Add 3 cups sifted powdered sugar, 1 cup at a time, blending after each addition. Add 6 tablespoons cocoa powder and 2 teaspoons oil; beat until smooth. Beat in about 1 tablespoon milk, if necessary, to make it easy to spread.

Apple Pancakes with Topping

1 cup all-purpose flour

¼ tsp. sugar

2 eggs

1½ cup milk

5 cups apples

1 stick margarine

½ cup dark brown sugar

Whipped dessert topping (optional)

1. Combine flour and sugar; make a well in the center. Beat eggs in a bowl; stir in milk. Add egg mixture to flour and stir until mixed. Pour batter in circles on a hot, lightly greased griddle; cook until lightly browned on both sides. Pancakes will be thin.

2. For topping, peel and slice apples. Put in pan with margarine. Cook on low heat until apples are tender. Add dark brown sugar and simmer until sugar dissolves; pour over pancakes. If desired, top with whipped topping.
Makes: 8 servings

Raspberry Ripple Crescent Coffeecake

¾   cup sugar

¼   cup butter, softened

2   eggs

¾   cup ground almonds

¼   cup all-purpose flour

1   tsp. grated lemon peel

1   8-oz. tube refrigerated crescent dinner rolls

8   tsp. seedless raspberry preserves

¼   cup sliced almonds

⅓   cup sifted powdered sugar

2   tsp. milk

1. Grease a 9×1½-inch round cake pan or 9-inch pie plate. In a small bowl, cream sugar, butter, and eggs until smooth. Stir in ground almonds, flour, and lemon peel; set aside. Separate crescent roll dough into 8 triangles. Spread 1 teaspoon of preserves on each triangle. Roll up, starting at shortest side of triangle and rolling to opposite point. Place rolls in prepared pan, arranging 5 rolls around outside edge and 3 in the center. Spread almond mixture evenly over rolls. Sprinkle with sliced almonds. Bake in a 375° oven for 22 to 32 minutes or until rolls are a deep golden brown and knife inserted in center comes out clean. Mix powdered sugar and milk; drizzle over cake. Serve warm.

Makes: 8 servings

Sour Cream Coffeecake

½   cup packed brown sugar

½   cup finely chopped nuts

1½   tsp. ground cinnamon

¾   cup butter, softened

1½   cups granulated sugar

1½   tsp. vanilla

3   large eggs

3   cups all-purpose flour

1½   tsp. baking powder

1½   tsp. baking soda

¾   tsp. salt

1½   cups sour cream

     Powdered Sugar Glaze

1. Grease bottom and sides of 10-inch tube pan or fluted cake pan. For filling, stir together brown sugar, nuts, and cinnamon; set aside. For cake, beat butter, granulated sugar, vanilla, and eggs in bowl with electric mixer on medium speed for 2 minutes, scraping bowl occasionally. Mix flour, baking powder, baking soda, and salt in another bowl. Beat flour mixture and sour cream alternately into sugar mixture on low speed until combined. Spread one-third of batter in pan; sprinkle with one-third of brown sugar mixture. Repeat twice. Bake in a 350° oven about 1 hour or until toothpick inserted in center comes out clean. Cool 10 to 15 minutes and remove from pan. Cool 10 minutes more. Drizzle with Powdered Sugar Glaze.

Makes: 12 servings

Powdered Sugar Glaze: Stir together ½ cup sifted powdered sugar, 2 to 3 teaspoons milk, and ¼ teaspoon vanilla.

Cream Puff Dessert

1   cup water
½   cup butter
1   cup all-purpose flour
6   eggs
2   pkgs. vanilla instant pudding mix
4   cups milk
1   8-oz. pkg. cream cheese, softened
1   12-oz. carton whipped dessert topping
     Chocolate syrup

1. Mix water and butter in a saucepan. Bring to a boil. Add flour all at once; stir rapidly until mixture forms a ball and leaves sides of pan. Remove from heat and cool. Beat in eggs one at a time, beating well after adding each egg. Spread on an ungreased jelly roll pan. Bake in a 400° oven for 30 minutes. Let cool on a wire rack.

2. Mix pudding mix with milk and beat well. Beat in softened cream cheese; spread over crust. Top with whipped dessert topping. Drizzle chocolate syrup on top and refrigerate for up to 6 hours.
Makes: 12 to 15 servings

Pumpkin Delight

1½   cups all-purpose flour
½   cup chopped nuts
¾   cup butter, softened
1   8-oz. pkg. cream cheese, softened
1   cup sifted powdered sugar
2   8-oz. cartons whipped dessert topping
2   pkgs. instant vanilla pudding mix
1   15-oz. can pumpkin
1½   cups milk
1½   tsp. pumpkin pie spice
½   cup chopped nuts

1. Combine flour, ½ cup nuts, and butter; press into a 13×9×2-inch baking pan. Bake in a 350° oven for 15 to 20 minutes until lightly browned; let cool. Mix cream cheese with powdered sugar. Fold in 1 carton whipped dessert topping and spread over first layer. Beat together pudding mix, pumpkin, milk, and ¾ teaspoon of the pumpkin pie spice until smooth; spread over second layer. Combine 1 carton whipped dessert topping and remaining ¾ teaspoon pumpkin pie spice. Fold in ½ cup nuts. Spread over third layer. Chill before serving.
Makes: 12 to 15 servings

Chocolate Mint Brownies

4   large eggs

2   cups sugar

1   cup all-purpose flour

1   cup unsweetened cocoa powder

1   cup butter, melted

1   tsp. vanilla

1   tsp. peppermint extract

¼   cup butter, softened

2¾   cups sifted powdered sugar

3   tbsp. milk

4   drops green food coloring

3   oz. unsweetened chocolate

3   tbsp. butter

1. Beat eggs lightly with a wire whisk. Add sugar and stir well. Combine flour and cocoa. Gradually stir into egg mixture. Stir in melted butter, vanilla, and ½ teaspoon of the peppermint extract; pour into greased 15×10×1-inch jelly roll pan. Bake in 350° oven for 15 to 18 minutes. Cake is done when toothpick inserted in center comes out clean.

2. Combine softened butter with powdered sugar. Stir in milk, remaining ½ teaspoon peppermint extract, and food coloring. Spread mixture over brownies. Put in freezer for 15 minutes. Combine chocolate and 3 tablespoons butter. Melt over low heat, stirring constantly; drizzle over the top of chilled bars.
Makes: 60 bars

Lemon Bars

1½   cups all-purpose flour

½   cup packed brown sugar

½   cup butter

1½   cups flaked coconut

1   cup chopped nuts

1   cup packed brown sugar

2   eggs

2   tbsp. all-purpose flour

½   tsp. baking powder

½   tsp. vanilla

¼   tsp. milk

1   cup sifted powdered sugar

1   tbsp. butter

   Juice of 1 lemon

1. For crust, combine 1½ cups flour, ½ cup brown sugar, and ½ cup butter; press into a 13×9×2-inch baking dish. Bake in a 275° oven for 10 minutes. Remove pan from oven. Increase oven temperature to 350°. For filling, combine coconut, nuts, 1 cup brown sugar, eggs, 2 tablespoons flour, baking powder, vanilla, and milk; pour over crust. Bake 20 minutes. For glaze, combine powdered sugar, 1 tablespoon butter, and lemon juice; drizzle over warm bars. Let cool on wire rack and cut into squares.
Makes: 36 bars

Cheesecake Brownies

1   cup butter, melted

2   cups granulated sugar

4   eggs

7   tbsp. unsweetened cocoa powder

2   cups all-purpose flour

2   tsp. vanilla

1   tsp. salt

2   8-oz. pkgs. cream cheese, softened

½   cup granulated sugar

1   egg

1   egg yolk

1½   tsp. lemon juice

1. Combine butter, 2 cups sugar, 4 eggs, and cocoa. Stir in flour, vanilla, and salt; spread into a greased 13×9×2-inch baking pan. Freeze for 10 to 15 minutes. Combine cream cheese, ½ cup sugar, 1 egg, egg yolk, and lemon juice; spread over frozen filling. Bake in 300° oven for 50 to 60 minutes.

Makes: 36 bars

Store cocoa powder in a glass jar in a cool, dry place.

Chocolate Crinkles

2   cups sugar

½   cup cooking oil

4   oz. unsweetened baking chocolate, melted and cooled

2   tsp. vanilla

4   large eggs

2   cups all-purpose flour

2   tsp. baking powder

½   tsp. salt

1   cup sifted powdered sugar

1. Mix sugar, oil, chocolate, and vanilla in bowl. Mix in eggs, one at a time. Stir in flour, baking powder, and salt. Cover and refrigerate for at least 3 hours.

2. Drop by spoonfuls into powdered sugar; roll around to coat. Shape into balls; place on greased cookie sheet and bake in a 350° oven for 10 to 12 minutes until edges are set.

Makes: about 36

Snowball Surprises

1   cup butter, softened
½   cup sugar
1   tsp. vanilla
2   cups all-purpose flour
1   cup finely chopped pecans
1   15-oz. pkg. chocolate kisses
    Sifted powdered sugar

1. In bowl, beat butter, sugar, and vanilla until light and fluffy. Add flour and pecans; mix well. Chill dough. Remove foil from candies. Form each cookie into a ball by shaping one tablespoon of dough around a kiss, covering the kiss completely. Place 2 inches apart on an ungreased cookie sheet. Bake in a 350° oven about 12 minutes until set but not brown. Transfer to a wire rack placed over waxed paper. While warm, sprinkle with powdered sugar. Store in covered container. These will taste best a day after baking.
Makes: about 36

the "SAUCEMAN" says

Chill cookie dough in refrigerator for 30 to 60 minutes before rolling it out. This reduces the amount of dusting flour or powdered sugar needed, which will make cookies less chewy.

Gingersnaps

1   cup packed brown sugar
¾   cup shortening
½   cup granulated sugar
¼   cup molasses
1   large egg
2¼   cups all-purpose flour
2   tsp. baking soda
1   tsp. ground cinnamon
1   tsp. ground ginger
½   tsp. ground cloves
¼   tsp. salt
     Granulated sugar

1. Mix brown sugar, shortening, granulated sugar, molasses, and egg in a bowl. Stir in flour, baking soda, spices, and salt. Cover and refrigerate for at least 1 hour. Lightly grease a cookie sheet. Shape dough into balls and dip into granulated sugar. Bake in a 375° oven for 10 to 12 minutes.
Makes: about 60

Candy Cookies

½ cup milk
½ cup butter
2 cups sugar
¼ cup unsweetened cocoa powder
  Dash salt
½ cup chunky peanut butter
1½ tsp. vanilla
3 cups quick-cooking oatmeal

1. Place milk and butter in a large microwave-safe bowl. Microwave on high for 1 minute. Add sugar, cocoa, and salt; mix well. Microwave on 100% power (high) for 4 to 6 minutes or until mixture boils, stirring occasionally. Stir in peanut butter and vanilla. Add oatmeal; stir until well mixed. Drop by teaspoons onto waxed paper. Let stand until cool and set.
Makes: about 48

To keep cookies fresh, place a piece of freshly baked bread in your cookie jar.

Cashew Cookies

¾ cup butter, melted
1 cup packed brown sugar
1 large egg
½ cup sour cream
½ tsp. maple syrup
2½ cups all-purpose flour
¾ tsp. baking soda
¾ tsp. baking powder
¾ tsp. salt
2 cups cashew halves
  Maple Syrup Frosting
  Cashew halves (optional)

1. Mix butter and brown sugar. Beat in egg, sour cream, and maple syrup. Stir in dry ingredients. Add cashew halves. Drop by tablespoons 2 inches apart onto a greased cookie sheet. Bake in a 350° oven for 8 to 10 minutes or until edges are firm. Cool on wire racks. Make Maple Syrup Frosting and frost cookies when they are cool. If desired, top each cookie with a cashew half.
Makes: about 48

Maple Syrup Frosting: Beat ½ cup softened butter and ½ teaspoon maple syrup until fluffy. Beat in 2 cups sifted powdered sugar and 2 teaspoons cream or milk for spreading consistency.

Just-Like-a-Brownie Cookies

1¼   cups butter

2   cups sugar

2   eggs

2   tsp. vanilla

¾   cup unsweetened cocoa powder

1   tsp. baking soda

½   tsp. salt

2   cups all-purpose flour

1   cup chopped walnuts (optional)

1. Cream butter and sugar. Add eggs and vanilla. Combine cocoa, baking soda, and salt; beat into butter mixture. Blend in flour. If desired, stir in walnuts. Drop 2 inches apart onto an ungreased cookie sheet. Bake in a 350° oven for 8 to 9 minutes or until edges are firm.
Makes: about 48

Cake Mix Cookies

1   2-layer pkg. desired flavor cake mix

2   eggs

½   cup cooking oil

½   cup chopped walnuts

1   cup semisweet chocolate chips (optional)

1. Combine cake mix, eggs, and oil until smooth. Stir in walnuts and, if desired, chocolate chips. Roll dough into walnut-sized balls. Place 2 inches apart on a greased cookie sheet. Bake in a 350° oven for 10 to 12 minutes or until edges are firm.
Makes: about 36

the "SAUCEMAN" says

Grease cookie sheets lightly. Too much grease will cause cookies to become thin and crisp.

Peanut Butter Cookies

1½ cups granulated sugar

1 cup packed brown sugar

1 cup peanut butter

1 cup shortening

2 large eggs

½ tsp. vanilla

3 cups all-purpose flour

1 tsp. baking soda

½ tsp. salt

1. Mix 1 cup of the granulated sugar, brown sugar, peanut butter, shortening, eggs, and vanilla in a bowl. Stir in flour, baking soda, and salt. Cover and refrigerate about 2 hours or until firm. Shape into 1-inch balls. Place 2 inches apart on an ungreased cookie sheet. Flatten balls with a fork dipped in remaining ½ cup granulated sugar, in a crisscross pattern. Bake in a 375° oven for 9 to 10 minutes or until edges are firm.
Makes: about 80

Mom's Chocolate Chip Cookies

1 cup Crisco

1 cup granulated sugar

1 cup packed brown sugar

2 eggs

1 tsp. baking soda

1 tsp. vanilla

½ tsp. salt

2 cups all-purpose flour

1 12-oz. pkg. semisweet chocolate chips

½ cup chopped walnuts

1. Combine Crisco, granulated sugar, and brown sugar until fluffy; beat in eggs. Mix in baking soda, vanilla, and salt. Stir in flour. Add chocolate chips and walnuts. Drop by spoonfuls onto an ungreased cookie sheet. Bake in a 350° oven for 10 to 12 minutes or until edges are lightly browned.
Makes: about 48

Sugar Cookies

1   cup butter

2   cups sugar

1   cup cooking oil

2   eggs

2   tsp. vanilla

5   cups all-purpose flour

2   tsp. baking soda

2   tsp. cream of tartar

   Sugar

1. Beat butter, sugar, and oil until fluffy. Beat in eggs and vanilla. Add flour, baking soda, and cream of tartar. Drop on a cookie sheet and flatten with a glass dipped in sugar. (Or, roll out one-third to one-half of the dough at a time on a lightly floured surface to ⅛-inch thickness and cut with a cookie cutter.) Bake in a 350° oven about 10 minutes or until edges just begin to brown. Cool on wire rack.
Makes: about 72

the "SAUCEMAN" says

Use a pizza cutter to easily cut cookie dough into pieces.

Thumbprint Cookies

½   cup butter, softened

¼   cup packed brown sugar

1   egg yolk

½   tsp. vanilla

1   cup all-purpose flour

¼   tsp. salt

1   egg white

1   cup flaked coconut

   Powdered Sugar Icing

1. Mix butter, brown sugar, egg yolk, and vanilla in a bowl. Stir in flour and salt until dough holds together. Shape dough into 1-inch balls. Beat egg white slightly. Dip each ball into egg white; roll in coconut. Place on an ungreased cookie sheet. Bake in a 350° oven for 8 minutes. Remove from oven. Press thumb in middle of each cookie and return to oven to bake for 3 minutes more. Fill thumbprints with Powdered Sugar Icing.
Makes: about 36

Powdered Sugar Icing: Stir together 1 cup sifted powdered sugar, ¼ teaspoon vanilla, and enough milk (2 to 3 teaspoons) to icing of desired consistency.

INDEX

INDEX

The charts on this page provide a guide for converting measurements from the U.S. customary system, which is used throughout this book, to the metric system.

Product Differences

Most of the ingredients called for in the recipes in this book are available in most countries. However, some are known by different names. Here are some common American ingredients and their possible counterparts:

- All-purpose flour is enriched, bleached or unbleached white household flour. When self-rising flour is used in place of all-purpose flour in a recipe that calls for leavening, omit the leavening agent (baking soda or baking powder) and salt.
- Baking soda is bicarbonate of soda.
- Cornstarch is cornflour.
- Golden raisins are sultanas.
- Green, red, or yellow sweet peppers are capsicums or bell peppers.
- Light-colored corn syrup is golden syrup.
- Powdered sugar is icing sugar.
- Sugar (white) is granulated, fine granulated, or castor sugar.
- Vanilla or vanilla extract is vanilla essence.

Volume and Weight

The United States traditionally uses cup measures for liquid and solid ingredients. The chart below shows the approximate imperial and metric equivalents. If you are accustomed to weighing solid ingredients, the following approximate equivalents will be helpful.

- 1 cup butter, castor sugar, or rice = 8 ounces = ½ pound = 250 grams
- 1 cup flour = 4 ounces = ¼ pound = 125 grams
- 1 cup icing sugar = 5 ounces = 150 grams

Canadian and U.S. volume for a cup measure is 8 fluid ounces (237 ml), but the standard metric equivalent is 250 ml.

1 British imperial cup is 10 fluid ounces.

In Australia, 1 tablespoon equals 20 ml, and there are 4 teaspoons in the Australian tablespoon.

Spoon measures are used for smaller amounts of ingredients. Although the size of the tablespoon varies slightly in different countries, for practical purposes and for recipes in this book, a straight substitution is all that's necessary. Measurements made using cups or spoons always should be level unless stated otherwise.

Common Weight Range Replacements

Imperial / U.S.	Metric
½ ounce	15 g
1 ounce	25 g or 30 g
4 ounces (¼ pound)	115 g or 125 g
8 ounces (½ pound)	225 g or 250 g
16 ounces (1 pound)	450 g or 500 g
1¼ pounds	625 g
1½ pounds	750 g
2 pounds or 2¼ pounds	1,000 g or 1 Kg

Oven Temperature Equivalents

Fahrenheit Setting	Celsius Setting*	Gas Setting
300°F	150°C	Gas Mark 2 (very low)
325°F	160°C	Gas Mark 3 (low)
350°F	180°C	Gas Mark 4 (moderate)
375°F	190°C	Gas Mark 5 (moderate)
400°F	200°C	Gas Mark 6 (hot)
425°F	220°C	Gas Mark 7 (hot)
450°F	230°C	Gas Mark 8 (very hot)
475°F	240°C	Gas Mark 9 (very hot)
500°F	260°C	Gas Mark 10 (extremely hot)
Broil	Broil	Grill

*Electric and gas ovens may be calibrated using celsius. However, for an electric oven, increase celsius setting 10 to 20 degrees when cooking above 160°C. For convection or forced air ovens (gas or electric), lower the temperature setting 25°F/10°C when cooking at all heat levels.

Baking Pan Sizes

Imperial / U.S.	Metric
9×1½-inch round cake pan	22- or 23×4-cm (1.5 L)
9×1½-inch pie plate	22- or 23×4-cm (1 L)
8×8×2-inch square cake pan	20×5-cm (2 L)
9×9×2-inch square cake pan	22- or 23×4.5-cm (2.5 L)
11×7×1½-inch baking pan	28×17×4-cm (2 L)
2-quart rectangular baking pan	30×19×4.5-cm (3 L)
13×9×2-inch baking pan	34×22×4.5-cm (3.5 L)
15×10×1-inch jelly roll pan	40×25×2-cm
9×5×3-inch loaf pan	23×13×8-cm (2 L)
2-quart casserole	2 L

U.S. / Standard Metric Equivalents

⅛ teaspoon = 0.5 ml	
¼ teaspoon = 1 ml	
½ teaspoon = 2 ml	
1 teaspoon = 5 ml	
1 tablespoon = 15 ml	
2 tablespoons = 25 ml	
¼ cup = 2 fluid ounces = 50 ml	
⅓ cup = 3 fluid ounces = 75 ml	
½ cup = 4 fluid ounces = 125 ml	
⅔ cup = 5 fluid ounces = 150 ml	
¾ cup = 6 fluid ounces = 175 ml	
1 cup = 8 fluid ounces = 250 ml	
2 cups = 1 pint = 500 ml	
1 quart = 1 litre	